MONET'S TABLE

Claude Monet c.1880.

In memory of Marguerite.
These lines are affectionately dedicated
to Kaki de Cossé-Brissac
for obvious reasons.

 Simon and Schuster
Simon & Schuster Building
Rockefeller Center
1230 Avenue of the Americas
New York, New York 10020

Originally published in French in 1989 under the title
Les Carnets de Cuisine de Monet
by Société Nouvelle des Editions du Chêne, Paris

English language edition first published in Great Britain
by Ebury Press, an imprint of Century Hutchinson Ltd.,
Brookmount House, 62-65 Chandos Place,
Covent Garden, London WC2N 4NW

English language edition edited by Alison Wormleighton
Translation by Pholiota Translations, London (Josephine Bacon)

Typeset in Great Britain by Saxon Printing Limited, Derby
Color separations by Actual of Bienne, Switzerland
Printed in Italy by Canale of Turin

10 9 8 7 6 5 4 3 2 1

Library of Congress Cataloging in Publication Data
Joyes, Claire.
    [Carnets de cuisine de Monet. English]
    Monet's table: the cooking journals of Claude Monet /
text by Claire Joyes; foreword by Joël Robuchon;
[translation by Josephine Bacon].
        p. cm.
    Translation of: Les carnets de cuisine de Monet.
    ISBN-13: 978-1-4165-4131-8
    ISBN-10:   1-4165-4131-4

    1. Cookery, French. 2. Monet, Claude. 1840-1926. I. Title.
TX719.J6513   1989
641.5944--dc20
                                           89-19695
                                            CIP

MONET'S TABLE
The Cooking Journals of Claude Monet

TEXT BY
Claire Joyes

PHOTOGRAPHS BY
Jean-Bernard Naudin

FOREWORD BY
Joël Robuchon

SIMON AND SCHUSTER

ACKNOWLEDGMENTS

The photographic record in this book could not have been completed without the help of many people. I would especially like to express my gratitude to all those who helped me so much, entrusting many items to me so that I could accurately recreate the atmosphere of Monet's home. These include the Cristalleries de St. Louis, Haviland & Parlon, Gérard Danton, Alain Fassier, Christian Benais, Jean-Pierre de Castro, Constance Maupin, Madeleine Gely, Hubert Brugière, Artémise & Cunégonde, Jean-Claude Romain, Pierre G. Bernard, Fanette, La Tuile à Loup, Au Bon Usage, Au Puceron Chineur, Eric Dubois, Madame Est Servie, Galerie Paramythiotis, Nathalie Mabille de Villers in Arthies, Fauchon, Cassegrain, Ercuis, and La Créperie at Villers-en-Arthies. My special thanks go to Madame Nathalie Révillon, manageress of Maxim's Traiteur, who prepared all the dishes for photography with a genuine concern for their authenticity and with so much enthusiasm.

Nanou Billaut

I would like to take this opportunity of thanking Monsieur Gérard Van der Kemp of the Institute, Curator of the Claude Monet Museum, Madame Gérard Van der Kemp, who was unstinting in her enthusiasm for this project, and Madame Claudette Lindsey for her efficient and generous assistance, as well as Madame Nathalie Mabille, and Mademoiselle Catherine Gourdain.

Claire Joyes

CONTENTS

FOREWORD

Having abandoned my native Poitou, I became a Parisian by adoption, to better practice the art I so loved. In 1980, while I was working as the *chef de cuisine* at the Hotel Nikko, I visited Claude Monet's house in Giverny; I remember the occasion very vividly.

The garden flowers blended into a harmonious color scheme and the decor and design of the painter's beautiful home were so innovative that I was greatly moved by them.

Inside the house, the large, chrome-yellow dining room left me with the impression of a lavishly run household. I very much liked the huge, simply decorated, blue-tiled kitchen with its array of equipment and utensils, which for me evoked the delicious food that had been so lovingly prepared here. Perhaps this is where I unconsciously conceived the idea of the future ideal restaurant.

That day, a thought suddenly came to me. Wouldn't it be wonderful to one day discover this family's culinary secrets, and to have the immense pleasure of

eventually recreating them? Now that Claude Monet's cooking journals have been revealed and published, thanks to Claire Joyes and Jean-Marie Toulgouat, this has actually become possible.

I very much enjoyed adapting the recipes, and have carefully checked them to make sure that you will have no difficulty in making these dishes.

In order to get to know the artist better and discover his personality through his lavish cuisine, I read a great deal, and this enabled me to get to know this giant among men, a great man who had been able to overcome all the vicissitudes of life.

His friends and biographers relate that he had a hearty appetite, but that he was discerning and even extremely fussy about food. For his many guests — including Clemenceau, Renoir, and Pissarro — and for his family, he carved game, roasts, and poultry himself at the table. He preferred foie gras from Alsace and truffles from Périgord. He adored fish, especially the pike from his own pond. He had a

kitchen-garden which was scrupulously maintained, and in which he grew herbs, aromatics, vegetables from the Midi, and field mushrooms which were carefully picked at dawn.

I was delighted by the discovery of the recipes, because they are a real palette of tastes, yet full of common sense, for use in the service of a simple, bourgeois and tasty cuisine. Some of them are extremely simple, others more difficult, requiring a certain amount of professionalism which was quite an achievement for the period. It should not be forgotten that none of the equipment was available which we find so indispensable today. Giverny did not even possess an ice-box!

For your inventiveness, for your great generosity, for all these beautiful and great recipes, for these precious journals, the evidence of the great cooking of the past, for this wonderful lifestyle,

Thank you, Claude Monet.

JOËL ROBUCHON
Chef de Cuisine
Restaurant Jamin, Paris

THE TASTE OF AN ERA

Autumn 1900.
Marthe's marriage to
Theodore Butler
brought family and
friends together for a
celebratory luncheon.

A Turn of the Century Table

"February 4, 1884.
Tasted a banana for the first time in my life,
I won't do it again until purgatory."

JULES RENARD, *DIARY.*

*I*f a house has character, the fact is obvious immediately. Claude Monet's house at Giverny certainly did, down to the smallest details of its kitchen. With its essentially bourgeois character, this house and its large, walled garden became for Monet a perfect haven. It was his own separate world, from which he drew continual inspiration for over 40 years.

Monet always retained the predilection for over-indulgence that was characteristic of the French middle class at this period, and Giverny provided a place where he could enjoy his taste for the good life to the full. This instinctive, physical enjoyment of life was also the basis for Monet's painting. For him, painting was never applied theory – it was a practical reality. Heedless of references to the past, he lived for the present; he was very much a man of his times.

Monet's cooking journals do contain a few faint traces of unconscious nostalgia, a flavor of the Restoration or the Second Empire, which, of course, was recent history in those days. Yet the journals mostly contain innovations of the Third Republic, combined with a few old favorites,

Opposite: At Giverny the place settings were prepared in the kitchen before the table was set.

Right: Claude Monet, *Luncheon on the Grass* (left-hand fragment), 1865-1866. Paris, Musée d'Orsay.

15

and seasoned with those exotic touches people have craved since ships conquered the spice route on the high seas.

Eating well was something to which Monet had always been accustomed. There is little information available about the meals that were eaten in the family home in Le Havre, where he spent most of his childhood. By all accounts, his boyhood was spent in bourgeois comfort. His father was in business as a supplier to the navy, and his mother is supposed to have been an excellent hostess and to have entertained her guests with after-dinner songs, as she had a very pretty voice. Monet was less than 20 years old when she disappeared, and all the memories of the rituals of Le Havre faded into oblivion with her.

In 1860, Monet drew an unlucky number in the lottery for selective military service and served with the Chasseurs d'Afrique regiment in Algeria. The landscape and light did not prove too harsh for his liking, and, in fact, he claimed that Algeria inspired the earliest of his visual impressions. Yet he never discussed the food he ate there. It is impossible to believe that he never tasted and enjoyed that aromatic cuisine, simmered in earthenware pots on rudimentary little hearths, those delicious dishes so skillfully cooked over charcoal.

Monet was only 20 when he went to North Africa, but he had already held exhibitions of his works and he had established friendships with Boudin, Pissarro, Cézanne, Courbet, and a number of other young men who were destined to become leading figures in the arts in the coming years.

After his return from Algeria in 1862, Monet began to work with Boudin, Jongkind, Renoir, Bazille, and Sisley. His rebellion against the art establishment was becoming apparent, and his family responded to his seeming intransigence by cutting off his allowance. Poverty began to bite, as he had as yet very little income from his work. But though accustomed to a degree of comfort, and passionate about his food, Monet was prepared to make any sacrifice, undergo any discomfort for the sake of his art.

It was at about this time, in the mid 1860s, that Monet painted Camille Doncieux. They began living together, had a child, Jean, and married in 1870. With the outbreak of the Franco-Prussian War, Monet went to England, where he was influenced by the paintings of Turner and Constable, and where he developed a taste for a number of English dishes. He returned to France the following year, via the Netherlands, discovering more dishes that were to remain firm favorites.

In 1871, Monet, Camille and Jean settled in Argenteuil, a village on the Seine near Paris, famous for its boating. They remained there for six years. This marked a turning point in Monet's life, the restless, poverty-stricken bohemian existence of the previous decade being replaced by stability and relative comfort. Though always short of cash and continually in debt, Monet had actually begun to earn a reasonable living from his paintings. He acquired a sailboat, which he used as a studio for painting trips on the river, pursuing his fascination with water. It was at the charming, vine-covered cottage in Argenteuil that Monet created his first garden, reflecting his lifelong delight in flowers. Here, too, no doubt, he was able to indulge his other great passion, food.

1874 was another landmark in Monet's life, when Monet and his friends, including Renoir, Sisley, Pissarro, Degas, and Berthe Morisot, staged their first group exhibition. In all, there were 165 canvases from about 30 artists. The uniformly hostile reaction of the press, who christened the group "Impressionists," was a clear indication of the resistance the new movement would encounter over the coming years.

Below: The annual Côte de Gaillon race was an occasion for this family of automobile enthusiasts and picnic-lovers to get together.

Above:
Veuve Clicquot
champagne was
often drunk at
Giverny.

Opposite: In
summer, the garden
was a riot of color.

From 1878 through 1881, Monet rented a house at Vétheuil, further down the Seine, about 40 miles from Paris. Camille was by this time very ill. Monet, Camille, Jean, and their second son, Michel, shared the house with Alice Hoschedé and her six children; Alice and her husband, former patrons of Monet, had recently been financially ruined and had separated. Following the death of Camille in 1879, the family lived as one, and Alice Hoschedé became Monet's second wife in 1892, after her estranged husband's death.

In his continuous struggle to impose his painting style, Monet was inhibited by the ever-present financial worries and the frustrating absence of a space large enough for him to work in comfortably. It was only at Giverny, which he discovered in 1883, that Monet was able to establish the lifestyle that really suited him. It was here that his ideas about food took shape, and Alice Hoschedé was to be their principal interpreter. Between them, Monet and Alice created their own art of living, something that today would be called style.

Their sole culinary ambition was to serve beautifully prepared dishes using whatever the kitchen-garden or the farmyard could supply. This was their food, homemade but often making use of recipes invented by the great restaurants they patronized, or even dishes created by their friends, who included writers, art collectors, painters and actors.

Many of the dishes can, of course, be

found in other cookbooks, but the recipe for the Monets' *bouillabaisse* came from Paul Cézanne, the recipe for their bread rolls from Jean Millet. Their *tarte Tatin* was a souvenir of their visits to the Tatin sisters themselves, to sample this famous dish. Origins such as these add zest to the dishes for us today, just as they undoubtedly did for the Monets a century ago.

Monet and Alice had decided to live out of town but not actually in the provinces. The house at Giverny was not one of those lonely country houses where one can relax far from the exhausting frenzy of the big city. Their life was a charming amalgam of a deliberately simple , rustic lifestyle, with all its attendant pursuits, combined with the tolerant, but totally independent attitude to life typical of the inhabitants of a vast metropolis. It was a rural idyll in which urban values had been transposed to the countryside.

In the magnificent era of fin-de-siècle France, eating habits were still somewhat in a state of confusion; the art of good living only emerged with difficulty after much trial and error. Haute cuisine was still in its infancy, and even the compilation of menus was of recent invention.

During this period, in which France's constitution changed more frequently than her eating habits, quantity reigned supreme. A few eccentrics – whom some complimented with the epithet "esthete," but who were, in fact, the precursors of our

modern dieticians – urged greater sobriety and discernment, but in vain.

It is remarkable how much was accomplished in matters of custom and taste in a relatively short time. This applies not only to eating habits but also to the ingredients. The dishes Monet so enjoyed, such as *soles à la normande,* were born at virtually the same time as he was.

T aste is a complex subject. Not only is it highly personal but it also must always be considered in context. For example, in 1888, the desserts which Monet and everyone else liked and which seem to us today to be rather heavy, such as the *galette de plomb* (a flat cake made with cream), featured in the menu served to President Carnot in the train which took him to the Dauphiné region. In an era that was rather slow-moving, when it took eight hours to travel by train to a town that today is only two hours away, this was a perfectly suitable menu. The same applies to the secret recipes of the Maison Dorée, the Café Anglais or Chez Hardy, which took their time to percolate down to the tables of the middle classes or along the length of the Seine Valley. In any case, local shops needed to be stocked, and the markets provisioned with the right ingredients.

Even though this style of cooking may

be complicated, requiring the mistress of the house to be a master of organization, what a reward it is to be served food that is fresh and in season!

From the vantage point of our modern age – in which Japanese dine in Paris with Venetians from London or Americans from Brussels – looking back on these more parochial times inevitably creates a certain

Below: Monet in his garden. Although he liked informal gardens, Monet did not entirely escape from the contemporary taste for formal landscaping.

nostalgia. In those days, green peas were not sent great distances if it could be helped because it was believed that they would lose their sweetness. There is alot of truth in this. We have come a long way from that lost luxury of freshness. Nevertheless, against all odds, a few diehards have continued to worship at the almost abandoned shrine of the "homemade."

The Rotunda Drawing Room

> "*And that bleached velum gilded by Clovis Eve*
> *Evokes who knows what faded charm*
> *The soul of their fragrance and the shadow their dream.*"
>
> HEREDIA

Some houses rule us more than we rule them. The shape of a room in the great Château de Rottenbourg was to throw everyone's life into confusion, for it was the rotunda drawing-room here that brought Monet and Alice together.

Paris at the time was in the grip of a frenzy. Albert Wolf wrote in *Le Figaro* that five or six rebels, including a woman – who was none other than Berthe Morisot – had become involved in an exhibition organized by the art dealer, Paul Durand-Ruel. The lurid details included the account of a man who had to be arrested at the exit because he was biting the passers-by. One hostile critic, seizing upon the unassuming title of Monet's painting, *Impression: Sunrise*, had christened the group "Impressionists." In fact, the label was so apt that it was quickly adopted by the artists themselves.

Every hostess who prided herself on being avant-garde vied for the company of these rebels. Ernest Hoschedé, an art-collector and patron of the arts to his very soul, was immune to this kind of flamboyance. But although he knew that Impressionist painting did not necessarily cause the beholder to fly into a rage, he had not yet discovered that painting in general can actually lead to one's downfall.

Alice, his wife, was an extremely well-heeled young lady. Her family, the Raingos, sold art bronzes and expensive clocks to the Royal courts of Europe, including the Tuileries Palace. They also reproduced Jacob Petit models and were, in effect, the "movers and shakers" in Belgian society in Paris. On her father's death, Alice had inherited the Château de Rottenbourg, located at Mongeron, in Normandy, and Ernest had devoted much time to refurbishing it. When it came to redecorating the large rotunda drawing-room, he thought of Monet. On that fateful September day in 1876, Monet was anxiously awaited and his arrival caused a sensation. It was this arrival which Blanche Hoschedé, Alice and Ernest's daughter, chose to recall in her all-too-brief memoirs.

Of course, no one detected the first crack which threatened the whole structure. Monet, who so loved the countryside, was penniless once again and had every reason to rejoice in the opportunity of exchanging his money worries for the serenity of spacious grounds in which to paint, and the carefree life at the château.

Opposite: The famous yellow waterlilies at the height of summer.

Pages 24-27: The garden in summer. Though near Paris, it was like being at the world's end.

The garden at Montgeron was a confusion of styles but displayed a certain gauche charm with its angular flower-beds, its Medici urns, and its romantic style of landscaping.

The Hoschedés were lavish hosts, and set a fast pace, literally driving their families crazy with the confusion in which they left their finances.

Ernest spent a lot of time in Paris, as busy unearthing rare art treasures as he was attending to his business affairs. Alice and her children spent more time at Rottenbourg; she loved it there. A socialite, quite excitable, very pious and something of a mystic, Alice was an attentive hostess and very lively, but sensitive, and easily tired. Today she might be described as a cyclical manic depressive. She loved the countryside but had great need for company; Rottenbourg, with its proximity to Paris, attracted many visitors.

Ernest was one of the first collectors of the new schools of painting for which he paid high prices because he was a generous man, as Monet knew only too well. Unfortunately, he had to part with a few of his treasures to ward off the abyss which was threatening to – and did eventually – engulf him.

At Montgeron, the Hoschedés lived a life which combined frivolity with intellectual pursuits and which could be considered avant-garde. Ernest, the ostentatious playboy, would bring his guests from the Gare de Lyon in Paris by private train. Ernest and Alice seemed to be living in a daydream. Life was a mad whirlwind, everything glittered, perhaps a little too much so.

The frequent visitors who were traditionalists mingled happily with those who were avant-garde. Impressionists such as Sisley, Manet, or Monet did not displace the family portraits, of which the most recent were signed by J.J. Henner, Carolus Duran, Benjamin Constant, and Baudry.

Carolus Duran was one of the traditionalist painters who frequented Montgeron. Carolus was amusing, had no doubts about anything, especially not himself, and he was quite right because he was extremely talented. He frequented numerous salons of which he was often the official portraitist. In fact, he has left us one of the rare existing portraits of Monet. He was incredibly charming, and fascinated everyone by his conversation which was something of a monolog. He danced, rode horses, sang, played the piano like everyone else, but also played the organ like James Tissot and was an excellent pistol shot. He lived quite close by and often came over to pay a neighborly call and enliven the evenings. He remained close friends with Monet.

On the avant-garde side, there was Georges Charpentier, the publisher, who founded *La Vie Moderne*, an excellent magazine condemned by its very quality to a short lifespan. Charpentier had the brilliant idea of organizing one-man shows of paintings at the magazine's offices, an extremely daring move for the times. Renoir exhibited there, as did Monet.

It was difficult to work in that atmosphere of a perpetual carnival. Yet Ernest, ever the attentive host, had thought of everything and a pavilion originally built as an orangery, away from the house, served Monet as a studio. In wanting to immortalize Rottenbourg, Ernest might almost have had a premonition.

He left it to Monet to choose the subject matter that seemed best to express the spirit of the place. Monet decided to decorate the rotunda drawing room with representations of the white turkeys who strutted through the park, the massed dahlias by the pool, and the pool itself. He later added a hunting scene, depicting figures in the undergrowth, including Ernest himself in the foreground.

Monet remained at Rottenbourg for a long time, and managed to produce a lot of work there, but it is not known if Camille ever came to join him. It was only when they returned to Paris that the Hoschedé and Monet families – parents and children – became really close friends. There is at least one park engraved in the memories of the youngest members of the family. It is the Parc Monceau in which Marcel Proust and the beautiful Bénardaky sisters would come to play a few years later, as described in Proust's *Remembrance of Things Past*.

While Monet was staying at Montgeron, Alice perceived the unmistakable signs of shaky finances. Ernest was spending less and less time at Rottenbourg and seemed to be increasingly preoccupied. She was gradually left more alone with her children, the servants and the company of an artist who produced very brilliant work. This gave her plenty of time in which to eventually compare her overgrown child of a husband with this simple but reliable man.

The specter of ruin hovered in the background. Nevertheless, Ernest, ever an enthusiastic supporter of the Impressionists, bought three new canvases from Monet in the following year, 1877. Then, in August of that year, he was declared bankrupt. The whole of that summer through September, passed in inventory-takings, court-ordered auctions, and other horrors. About 50 Impressionist paintings in his collection were sold, all at ridiculously low prices. The twelve canvases by Monet were sold at an average of only 184 francs each.

After some terrible tribulations including some humiliating episodes, the ruined Hoschedés with their six children, Marthe, Blanche, Suzanne, Jacques, Germaine and Jean-Pierre, plus a housemaid, governess and cook moved in with Camille and Claude Monet – who were themselves impoverished – at Vétheuil.

LIFE AT GIVERNY

Monet and Butler
waiting to be
driven to market,
an important
weekly ritual in the
household.

Pride of Place

"From the debris of the palace
I built my cottage."

SULLY PRUD'HOMME

Above: This black-and-white photo shows how the house was shrouded in luxuriant vegetation.

Camille died at Vétheuil after a lengthy illness, and Alice and Ernest were separated. It will never be known whether it was courage or a wider vision that motivated Madame Hoschedé, who was so conventional, so religious, and who valued respectability so highly, to share her life with Monet and bring up his two sons, Jean and Michel.

They arrived at Giverny in late April and early May, 1883, with their eight children, the youngest of whom was less than five years old. The move had been expensive and was staggered over a period

Opposite: The entrance hall at Giverny.

of about six days, punctuated with the financial disruptions which had surreptitiously entered their everyday lives. They had a vast horde of possessions, which were brought down the Seine in their four boats. However, their baggage included the best of weapons with which to confront the unknown, a magnificent appetite for life, supported by an almost unconscious ability to rapidly forget the past. On their way down, they had shed their cook, their governess, and even Alice, that generous housemaid who had insisted on remaining in their service without wages after Rottenbourg had been sold.

Alice Hoschedé had been used to a life of great affluence, and she had now committed herself to an impoverished artist. This showed much daring on her part, especially in view of the age in which she lived. She now exchanged Rottenbourg in favor of a simple, converted farmhouse.

In truth, Monet and Alice were unaware of their good fortune, because the real luxury of Giverny was the fact that they had no close neighbors, and that they were the lucky owners of a walled garden. This type of garden not only makes the best use of microclimates, it is also an excellent way of guaranteeing privacy.

In reality, Monet could not have found a better retreat than this elongated house, called the Maison du Pressoir (House of the Cider Press), which was so quickly transformed, rendered slightly more bourgeois with fairly successful results. It had a good north-south aspect, and overlooked a garden sloping gently down to wide meadows – which at that time of year were a sea of flowers and plants. Next to the meadows lay a field of wild irises, overshadowed by ancient pollarded willows. The fruit-trees which covered the hills were in blossom; a delightful little train puffed along between the river and the narrow, twisting road at the bottom of the garden, known as the Chemin du Roy (the King's Way); and the washing-stones down by the water were a meeting-place where the village women could exchange gossip.

So close to Paris, yet one was at the world's end!

They couldn't afford an architect to work on the house, so they restricted themselves to straightforward alterations. Both Monet and Alice were aware of the benefits of planting new vines and rambling roses, which will hide and beautify the ugliest of walls. There were a lot of outhouses: basements, cellars, shacks, all of them absolutely essential for the running of the household.

Although the countryside was so lovely, the same could not be said of the garden Monet had inherited, with its conifers and its rigidly geometrical layout. It lay in the midst of the orchard of plum-trees which looked so promising that year. This must have been the subject of some interesting conversations with Monet's friends, the artist Caillebotte and the playwright Mirbeau.

There was still enough room for plants with which to decorate the house and supply the table. Monet, helped by his children, immediately began sowing aromatics and flower seeds, so as to have something to pick for painting when the weather was bad. They planted annual chrysanthemums, poppies and large sunflowers. For the table, there was still time from July through September to grow romaine lettuce, spinach, peas, and radishes. Time was short, and they had so much to do, making themselves comfortable and starting to paint.

They did not yet know that, by the time the flowers had taken up all the available space, they would be able to acquire another garden as big as the first, the large garden attached to the Maison Bleue (the Blue House) in the village, which would become their kitchen-garden.

As for their beloved boats, they had set

their sights on a mooring at the Ile aux Orties (Nettle Island), an island in the Seine, where the rowboat, the two mahogany skiffs and the studio-boat were tied up. They were certain that this island would belong to them one day, and it features in many canvases painted at Giverny. Monet posed Suzanne, Alice's daughter, on it to paint *the Lady with a Parasol*. Monet and Alice set to work at once making improvements, because there was something about the place which would otherwise make you die of boredom if you did not take action. Yet how could these people who had recently been so impoverished suddenly start to rebuild Babylon? The answer is very simple. In addition to the Impressionists' admirers, who were more numerous than has been acknowledged, there was a person in Paris to whom they owed almost everything, although they never thought of it that way.

This was Paul Durand-Ruel – a man whose family had begun to doubt his sanity. Durand-Ruel was a businessman, as well as a patron of the arts, and he did some banking and financing on the side. Durand-Ruel, the "Monsieur Durand" referred to by Renoir, Sisley, Pissarro, Monet, and everyone else, was certainly not indifferent to making money, but he took the ultimate risk of acquiring canvases by all these artists. He advanced them the funds they needed for survival, although sometimes

Page 36-37: The kitchen was painted in brilliant pale blue to match the tiles. The kitchen and the studio were the two sacrosanct rooms of the house.

the paintings he bought from them had not even left the studio. He thus acquired hundreds of paintings which were difficult to sell, since it is always hard to be ahead of one's time. Monet's creditors would present themselves at the gallery and Durand-Ruel would settle the cost of schooling for the children, settle the accounts of the artists' materials supplier, and the framer, and even pay Monet's tailor. Monet always dressed well whatever his financial circumstances.

That is how the pinkish-ocher roughcast exterior came to be darkened, the gray shutters repainted in Neti green, similar in color to Veronese green, and a long, wooden balcony built to run the length of the house. A new kitchen was added over the cellar and a suite of two rooms over the barn, which had been transformed into a studio. The kitchen and the studio, two sacrosanct spots, were the first to be subjected to major remodeling.

Monet and Blanche decided on pale colors for the walls, pastel tones, except in the dining-room which was painted in pale and medium chrome yellow. The dining-room led into a blue room. Whether one opened the door of the kitchen, the small entrance-hall or the mauve drawing-room, there was an escalation, a progression, of color from cobalt blue, through madder to white. All these hues were created by Monet and were the subject of lengthy discussions with the village house-painter,

who took a while to recover from his astonishment! The staircases, narrow corridors, and the two dressing-rooms, as well as the bathroom with its huge, friendly copper water-heater, were painted in a more English color scheme of white, offset here and there by a touch of blue or madder. The girls' rooms were more acid in tone.

Finally, there was the suite of rooms occupied by Alice and Monet. They overlooked a lovely little hill which served them as a natural barometer, bathed as it often was in a bluish, opalescent haze, the poetic counterpart of the barometer on the wall which Monet was never without. The walls were adorned with damask tablecloths sewn together.

Above: Blue-leaved waterlilies in the pond.

Opposite:
The ancient
ice cream maker,
which was essential
equipment for
making the banana
ice cream served on
Christmas Day.

The kitchen, which was to be constantly modernized, has been handed down to us in the state which was the ultimate in rural comfort just prior to World War I. The walls and ceiling sparkled with a bright-blue gloss paint, which matched the blue Rouen tiles. These were to be found in all the local kitchens, just as it was the custom in this part of the country to tile the chimneypieces. Nothing could be a better complement to the array of copper pots and pans than those plain little Rouen tiles. The white porcelain hanging lamp would take over from the daylight which streamed in through the windows, unhindered by any curtains. That monolithic monument, the stove – the alter on which so many flavors depend – had pride of place.

Florimond's Kitchen-Garden

*"At present, lowly guardian of fruits and salads
I defend this enclosure against marauders..."*

JOSÉ MARIA DE HEREDIA

It is the habits of a lifetime that determine whether a house will survive, prosper or decline. But, half a century later, it is virtually impossible completely to unravel chains of events – to pinpoint exactly when particular habits crept in, or to analyze how those imperceptible changes occurred which give places their character and style.

Above: Claude Monet, *Still Life with Melon*, 1876. Gulbenkian Museum.

Opposite: Peaches were grown in the kitchen-garden run by Florimond.

Although Monet took an interest in everything, and was certainly not one to retire into an ivory tower, Alice and the two daughters who succeeded her, Marthe then Blanche, ran the house according to a host of immutable rituals. What is disconcerting is their Benedictine-like adherence to a strict timetable at Giverny (make no mistake, the true Benedictine of the place

41

was Monet), even though the recreation each day was itself relatively carefree. The activities might fluctuate between, say, observing the rose-beetles who lived exclusively on a diet of rose-leaves in the garden, "tinkering with bicycles" (as Alice described the boys' persistent experiments with mechanical inventions), canoeing, photography, picnics, plus lessons in Latin and botany from the local parish priest Abbé Toussaint.

The family's time was occupied in a private life that was very affectionate and loving, even demanding. There were live-in staff who were integrated into a clearly defined emotional background, which was both close and distant at the same time. Some individuals would control a particular domain. There was naturally a succession of gardeners and cooks, and they had to know how to prepare the kind of food that Monet liked and landscape his garden in the way he envisaged it.

Right: Claude Monet, *The Basket of Grapes,* Paris. Private collection.

Below left: Germaine and Sisi leaving for a picnic on the Ile aux Orties (Nettle Island).

Thus, Marguerite (whom the author knew well) presided over the kitchen, Félix over the garden, and Sylvain over the wine-cellar, the studio, and above all the cars. Paul was responsible for various missions of trust, while Florimond ruled the kitchen-garden.

The farmyards were only a few steps away from the blue-painted kitchen. Some turkeys were raised here, goodness knows why, but they were not white like those at Rottenbourg. Turkey-rearing was soon abandoned, however, because they are not very dainty creatures, and no one in the household liked eating turkey. Nevertheless, it was amusing to have some farm animals around.

The upper farmyard, which was reserved for the ducks, had a pond in which they could dabble. Nearby, there was another pond for watering, and a nesting-

tree, as well as clumps of shrubbery, because ducks like to keep their nests hidden away. This little enclosure was home to Nantes ducks and White Indian Runners, whose females were excellent layers, but might be outdone by the Khaki Campbells. There were also some exquisite little Mandarin ducks which had been bought for the sole pleasure of looking at them. Barbary and Rouen ducks were banned, however, since they were considered to be too greasy.

Monet was so fanatical about the poultry he was served at table that he took an inordinate amount of time choosing ducks and hens to be used for breeding stock. He haunted the breeders and bird-sellers, because he considered the local farmers to be too unselective in their breeding techniques.

In the hen yard, where three or four different breeds were being reared, the situation was quite complicated. Houdans, who were sought after for their laying capacity as well as their flesh, clucked away with beautiful white Gâtinaise hens and plump black Bresse hens, and there were also a few Cayenne hens that had been presented as gifts by friends. These were sometimes joined by the odd pheasant.

The job of running the farmyard is usually that of the gardener, but it was Blanche who throughout her life, whenever she could, fed the ducks and hens. Although Paul, Marguerite's husband, had

Above: In the summer, the nasturtiums invaded the avenue leading to the front door.

been promoted to valet and butler, he would remove the eggs, supervise the rearing, and keep things tidy. He had to try to maintain order among the different breeds, stopping the Faverolles hens from dethroning the Houdan dynasties. He even had to keep a sort of hall of records, because certain breeds require the careful selection of roosters to keep their egg-laying performance high, which is very important in winter.

Fortunately, Monet detested domesticated rabbit and would only eat hare and wild rabbit, so there were no hutches. Nor were there dovecotes, because pigeons were bought from Duboc or Ledanois. There were so many different types of farm in the area that they did not lack suppliers.

Next to the second studio, which Monet had erected near the lime trees, there was an aviary. It was little more than a sickbay for unusual or wounded birds, and here all sorts of boarders were accommodated. These included the gulls sent from Belle-Ile by Monet for the "little ones," that is, Michel and Jean-Pierre, who would thus have an excellent excuse for going fishing. After all, the gulls needed feeding.

*U*ndoubtedly, a powerful spirit of organization breathed through this household, in which no good food was possible without a kitchen-garden. In this respect, the kitchen-garden was a work of art, one of the things of which Monet was justifiably most proud. In his mind, this vegetable garden was inseparable from the other things that to Monet were part of the good life – his flower-garden, the farmyards, a well-aged wine bottled by Sylvain, a well-cut suit, Marguerite's excellent cooking, and a good read in the studio-drawing room.

The two-and-a-half acre walled kitchen-garden, which stood at the opposite end of the village, in the rue du Chêne, was the exact counterpart of the flower-garden. Both had the same aspect, receiving the sun all day, and both were terraced in the same style. However, the

Above: The house in summer with the garden in full bloom.

Opposite: Preparing pike with white butter sauce for Sunday lunch (recipe on page 157).

slope of the kitchen-garden was steeper, and it was squarer, which made the arrangement of the sections easier and more attractive.

Everything that was banned from the flower-garden was strongly advocated here in the kitchen-garden. There was a strict geometrical plan and paths were laid out in straight lines, to allow the work to be carriedly out logically, rapidly and with minimum effort.

Doyenne de Comice and Beurré d'Hardempont pear-trees were espaliered along the sunny walls. Separated from them by a little path there were horizontally strung espaliers for "the apple harvest" of the Reine des Reinettes russets required for the upside-down apple tart, *tarte Tatin*. Few trees are needed in a kitchen-garden. The only ones allowed in Monet's were the long- and short-stemmed Montmorency cherry trees, as well as greengage plum-trees and Petite yellow plum-trees. These fruits were used by Marguerite to make her famous brandied preserves and the compotes of cherries preserved in their own juice. A few quince-trees and some ornamentals had also been planted.

Along with the garden in the rue du Chêne, Monet had purchased the house attached to it, known as the Maison Bleue (the Blue House). Florimond was installed here. He frequently needed the help of one or two gardeners from the main garden because the fruit and vegetable harvest was so abundant, to say nothing of the meticulous irrigation which had to be performed with the aid of an ill-tempered pump that made the devil of a noise.

A variety of cultivated plants grew side by side, native plants being cultivated right next to those from warmer climates. The space available was by no means too large considering the demanding nature and large appetites of the family.

Monet bought seeds and plants every-where he went, bartering with other gardeners ; he adored trying to grow the most delicate shoots as if to challenge the climate at Giverny. It was he who leafed through the catalogs and ordered from them.

He also insisted on the age-old custom that the garden be laid out with root vegetables, leaf vegetables, bulbs and seeds each grouped in their own section. Perfect order was the rule, even down to the arrangement of the cold-frames, the pyramids of pots for planting out melons, and the piles of cloches. There were trenches for Jerusalem artichokes, grown mainly as aromatics, and rows in which certain vegetables had to be grown, such as the red cabbage for which Monet had a passion.

All this denoted an absolute and disciplined layout worthy of a zoning map. There was no shortage of right-angles here! One could stroll along paths lined with climbing vegetables, along avenues of Milan cabbages, brussels sprouts, or broccoli, beside rows of romaine lettuces, celery, pale endives or Paresseux de Castillon spinach. One crossroads, which was marked by a rosemary bush, was bordered with thyme, chives, and savory for the lima beans, and even Belleville garlic for the *sauce verte*. Sage and oregano, with their blue flowers, dotted the edges of the path. Tarragon, however, cannot be grown to order; wherever it wants to develop it should be left to itself.

The sheltered, terraced area was

Opposite: Monet and his daughters-in-law with the first American painters to visit Giverny.

Pages 48–49: Although the layout of the garden at Giverny was geometric, this was obscured by the colorful, lush borders.

reserved for plants from more southern climes. There were red, yellow, and cherry tomatoes, Vert de Provence globe artichokes to be eaten raw when young, chili peppers, sweet peppers, Nice zucchini, all of them unknown in this region, as well as lima beans and green beans, rocamboles (a member of the onion family), and oriental garlic, and those little Egyptian pearl onions which taste so delicious when pickled in vinegar. Florimond was an expert in growing Chinese artichokes, a vegetable Monet loved. He was also very proud to bring his early vegetables to the kitchen from mid-February.

Florimond knew Monet's rages if the vegetables were not picked at the right time, yet nothing was more difficult. Every day, Monet would select from the vegetables ordered the previous day, and on Sunday he would choose those for the stockpot, which was indispensable for the preparation of soups and broths for the whole week.

The seed catalogs Monet so often studied were soon to become the relics of a vanishing era – a time when Paris grew almost everything it needed on its own doorstep, before those fields of cultivated blooms in the market-gardens and every kind of small farm were swamped under a rising tide of buildings and factories.

LIFE WITH MONET AND ALICE

Menu for the
wedding luncheon
of Germaine
Hoschedé and
Albert Salerou.

The Family Table

*"I have built my home among humans
but no sound of a horse nor a carriage matters to me
— How is that possible?
— To a distant heart, everything is a retreat."*

TAO YUANMING

had no particular vocation, organized the work of all the servants, and was hostess to relatives, Monet's friends, and the art-dealers. Like all those who are familiar with the ways of the world, she knew how to modulate her attitude, her vocabulary, and her menus to suit her guests. There were those who needed to be impressed a little and others where this would have been insensitive. With the natural simplicity and good taste of the upper classes, Alice was a master of the art of spending a fortune on things that were hardly noticeable.

A typical day in Alice's domestic life was dominated by a host of diverse duties. She would consult Monet when compiling the week's menus, at the same time taking account of the particular likes and dislikes of the lunch guests. She had to arrange with the cook the daily deliveries of vegetables from their kitchen-garden at the other end of the village.

Then there was the linen to be sorted out with Delphine, the maid, the curtains to arrange for her to iron, and some alterations to discuss with the seamstress.

An invisible barrier separated Alice and Monet's domain from the village. On one side of it, Giverny went about its business, while, on the other, Monet's home breathed to the rhythm and pace of the ancient ritual of cultivating the soil.

Alice ran the household, tolerated Monet's bad temper, raised eight children who

Opposite and above: The table set for Sunday lunch. The blue Japanese-inspired Creil china was used for most meals.

53

Alice also had to make out the shopping lists. Saturday was devoted to shopping. Sylvain would appear and take her to market at nearby Vernon. He himself was often given other tasks. He had to buy fresh bread and newspapers every day, run to a market-gardener who had a farm shop at Limetz to get some good asparagus, and search the watercress-farms of Saint-Marcel for that delicious watercress which features in the coat of arms of the town of Vernon. He might also need to buy some piece of kitchen equipment.

Alice had to remember to ask the floor-polisher to pay a visit. There was the store-room to restock, and the so-called spice-rack, a huge Régence-style cupboard stocked with the most precious preserves, tea from Kardomah, Salon de Provence olive oil, and spices such as cayenne pepper, saffron, paprika, cinnamon, and cumin.

The morning would thus pass with lightning speed. It was always a surprise to hear the little train passing, such a useful device for regulating one's watch. The train was always on time even if, as often happened, it was delayed by their boys having hoisted their canoes on board to avoid having to pass through several locks. In any case, it was high time the boys were home, as Monet would be back at eleven, impatient to sit down to lunch and a demon for punctuality. A first then a second stroke of the gong would assemble the scattered family in the dining-room for lunch, which

Opposite: Claude Monet, *The Luncheon*, 1868. Frankfurt, Stadt Institut. The painting shows Camille and Jean at the table, with Monet's place in the foreground.

Below right: Monet photographed by Sacha Guitry.

Pages 56-57: The breakfast table. This meal was a hodgepodge of habits learned from trips to Britain and the Netherlands.

was served at 11:30 precisely. Monet would cough irritably on the very half-second, causing panic in the kitchen.

The reason the family lunched so early was to allow Monet to make the best use of the light to work on his afternoon subject. Often rising before dawn, he would consult the hill he used as a natural barometer from his bedroom window, hoping to find it enveloped in a bluish haze, which would herald a fine day.

Next he would take a cold bath – under the watchful eye of Cézanne's *Nègre*, which hung in his dressing-room. He would then come down to the dining-room

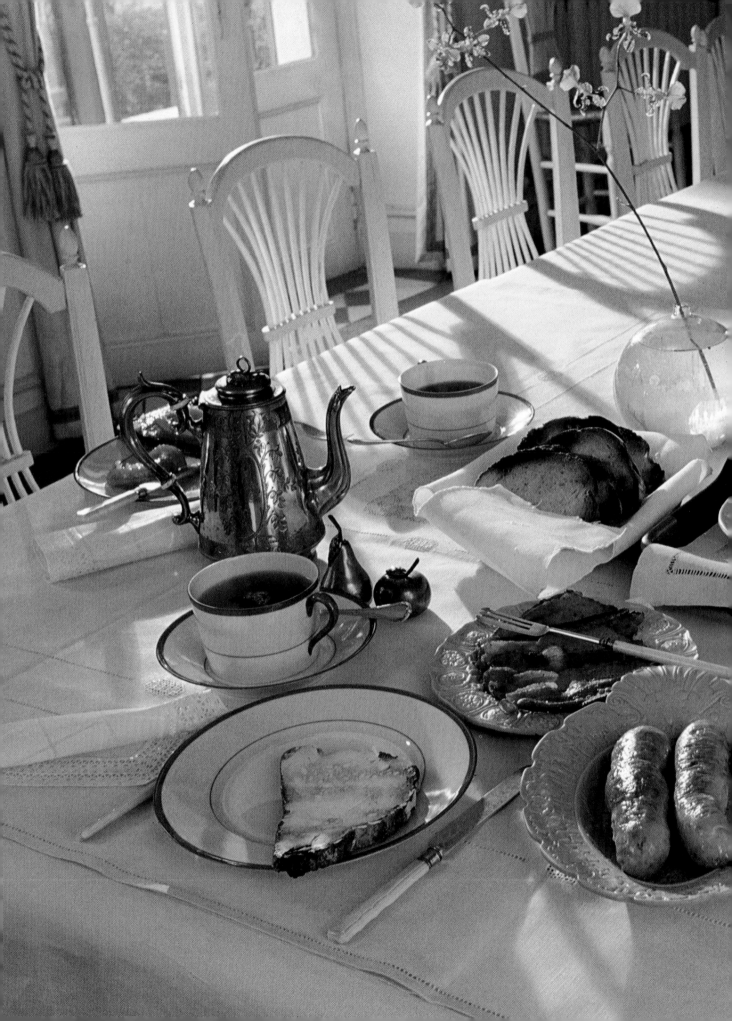

where a hearty breakfast awaited him. Monet would usually eat breakfast with Blanche, his step-daughter, who was also a painter, and who would enter with a wheelbarrow full of his canvases and easels for that day's subject. Then they were off through the countryside to the river to board their studio-boat, leaving the awakened house behind them, the day always full of little events to be recorded.

This first meal of the day was actually a hodgepodge of customs gleaned from trips to England and the Netherlands and, of course, from all those inns at which Monet had stayed when he was painting in the French countryside.

Above: Monet's desk as it might have looked in his lifetime.

Right: Monet, c. 1920, in the large studio, where he was painting the *Waterlily Decorations* for the Tuilerie Gardens Orangerie.

Familiar, happy sounds would emanate from the kitchen, where the oven was being lit, while they sat down to eggs and bacon, grilled tripe sausages, and Dutch or Stilton cheese, with toast and orange marmalade, and tea.

Fortunately, over the years, there were enough variations in the daily routine to shake the family out of this way they had of making time stand still.

As Monet had risen so early and worked from five or six o'clock in the morning, often in the wet, lunch at 11:30 was a welcome moment of relaxation which everyone found particularly important. It was also the meal to which guests were invited; the Monets never considered inviting people to dinner. This was largely because of the hour at which Monet retired. He would go to bed by 9:30 at the latest to be fresh for the next day's work. If he had to go any later, he would be completely out of sorts.

In fact, in one of his letters, probably written from La Creuse, Monet recounts, as if he were talking about a major disaster, that he had to dine at ten o'clock at night after going to hear his friend, the poet Maurice Rollinat, sing in the church at Fresselines.

A table set with the attractive blue china and the prospect of a good lunch would put him in a charming frame of mind – except on the days when he was dissatisfied with his painting! The family would often discreetly observe the way in which he entered the house and try to judge from his gait whether or not he was in a good temper.

In general, it was safest to serve food that was nothing less than delicious. Monet was such a fanatic about the right time for picking the vegetables that he would terrorize Florimond and his acolytes, and he could even burst into a rage over a sauce. Curiously, he would never reprimand the cook but would charge the mistress of the house with doing so.

This dining-room, in which the family portraits adorning the walls had been replaced by Japanese colored woodcuts of landscapes and figures, was the scene for some incidents which sometimes smacked of the burlesque. For instance, there was the tragi-comical day when Marguerite made a mistake in her banana ice cream recipe, and realized at the last moment that she was about to serve an ice cream flavored with kitchen salt. Everyone had a good laugh over it – 20 years later!

Like everyone else, Monet had his particular habits, and preferences, as well as some rather interesting eccentricities.

For instance, although Paul would serve at table, in his striped waistcoat, Monet revived a very ancient custom – one which had been taken very seriously by the gastronome Grimaud de la Reynière. He would carve the meat himself, at table, cutting up any kind of game, poultry or roast. For duck, he perfected a ceremony of his own devising. He would remove the wings, sprinkle them with nutmeg, freshly ground pepper and coarse salt and hand them over to Paul, who would take them into the kitchen to broil under the hottest flame imaginable.

As for salads, whether they were of

chicory laced with garlic and croutons, or dandelions with strips of fat bacon or purslane, Paul would present him with the large serving-spoon which he would fill with freshly ground pepper and coarse salt and dip in olive oil, adding a drop or two of wine vinegar. Paul would then pour the contents of the spoon over the salad and toss it. It would be black with pepper and inedible for anyone except Monet or Blanche, who loved anything that he did. That is why there were always two bowls of salad. The same applied to asparagus, which he liked barely cooked: two separate dishes were needed.

In the wine-cellar, which was run by Sylvain, the local rotgut was banned.

Above: Monet liked to add a whole spoonful of pepper and salt to a salad, so there was one bowl for him and Blanche, and another for everyone else.

Opposite: The house glimpsed through the trees.

Pages 62-63: The Sunday lunch table. Lunch began at exactly 11:30 A.M. every day.

Although Monet did not regard himself as a wine connoisseur, he did like fine wines, such as the burgundy recommended by Pissarro or the claret discovered by Durand-Ruel. He did not, however, disdain the minor vintages of the Loire and the rather harsh Chanturgue wine in which kidney beans were cooked. Monet cared little for champagne, which, at his table, was served decanted like ordinary wine.

After dinner, coffee was served in the studio drawing-room, after which the family devoted itself to the ritual of the homemade plum brandy poured into little round glasses which had been brought back from Norway. A few other bottles lined the little glass-fronted cabinet – homemade blackcurrant wine, marc (white brandy) brought from his native Berry by Paul and, for the ladies, exotic liqueurs from the French colonies (which were as often as not manufactured in Bordeaux).

Monet never lingered over his food. The service was quick and he even gave the order never to hand dishes around twice when his American step-son-in-law, Theodore Earl Butler, was lunching with them, because his slow eating habits drove Monet crazy.

After the meal, Alice and her daughters would withdraw to the mauve drawing-room, which was also the library. Monet would go back to work until the two strokes of the gong interrupted him for seven-o'clock dinner.

Picnics and Celebration Lunches

*"From the car, one barely has the leisure to
compare different types of foliage. And one cannot
see the flowering hedgerows... The trees that fly
away, they are trees, nothing more... they gallop by."*

MIRBEAU, *THE 628–E8*

Above: Traditional fare at the picnic marking the opening of the hunting season included *pâtés en croute* and terrines.

Opposite: A full lunch table, complete with glasses for wine, was set in the open air for the family's numerous picnics.

Little by little, even if their spirit lingers on, things change. There was the garden in which Monet worked so unstintingly and which he landscaped so brilliantly. There were the picnic baskets and the secret ritual of picking morels, the hunting parties, and the trips to Paris. There was the arrival of Caillebotte or Mirbeau who had come by boat down the Seine, and, of course, the steady stream of visitors as the summer progressed. They would manage to penetrate the barrier that had to be built around Monet to protect his work. Yet all this gradually dissolved and metamorphosed.

The household – which was run to the rhythm of its own seasons, punctuated with exhibitions of Monet's work – saw the children grow up and marry, and eventually saw the serenity of its garden disturbed by the games of four grandchildren. With the turn of the century, the time came for walks with Lily, Suzanne's daughter (who became Jean-Marie Toulgouat's mother) in the cart drawn by the nanny-goat. The garden was filled with the sounds of children, from the roaring of Lily's brother Jim's toy tigers, to the wailing of the dolls owned by Germaine's daughters Sisi and Nitou, from thirty-second crises to peals of laughter.

A second studio was therefore built near the lime-trees, just as a third studio would be erected in 1916 at the opposite end of the property.

A garage was erected next to the bicycle shed, which was cluttered with a whole arsenal of fishing-rods and nets of every

kind – shrimping-nets, nets for holding big fish, and double-meshed nets for catching eels in the River Rû. The garage, which even had a pit, was for Michel and Jean-Pierre, who loved to invent various pieces of diabolical, clanking machinery.

Gradually, automobiles replaced the carriages bringing visitors to and from the Hotel Baudy, the café which had become a hotel to cater for the increasing number of artists making pilgrimages to Giverny.

Monet never took the trouble to learn to ride a horse or a bicycle, much less to drive a car, but the two boys delightedly interpreted the moods and rumblings of the engine of the family's first Panhard-Levassor, which would change so many of their habits. It is difficult to imagine today the fever which gripped the family when they visited the earliest Paris car shows. The first Panhard was followed by another and joined by the Bonnet-Zédel, and the boys' Hotchkiss. Then there was that wonderful Zebra, the van which Sylvain used for going shopping. The day was still far off when the garage would house Michel's off-road vehicle, which was specially designed for crossing the Sahara.

The Abbé Toussaint officiated at the marriage ceremony of another of Alice's children, Suzanne. The household would

Pages 66-67: The basket contains cèpes, chanterelles and oyster mushrooms. A mushroom-picking foray was an excellent excuse for a picnic.

henceforth include an American son-in-law (Jean-Marie's grandfather), as well as a Norwegian daughter-in-law (Jacques's wife). It was also about to encompass a son-in-law (Germaine's husband) from Monaco, and another daughter-in-law (Jean-Pierre's wife), from Périgord. After the ceremony, there was a luncheon, the menu for which has been preserved; it was served in the studio-drawing-room. Four rows of paintings overlooked the guests as they dined. The rest of the day was spent in conversation around the pond. On this day of all days, nothing would induce one to forget to feed the goldfish.

Following the Monet-Rodin exhibition of 1889 at Georges Petit's gallery, the names of these two artists were on everyone's lips, and the family was able to live a more affluent lifestyle.

The famous exclamation of their friend, Georges de Bellio, "Et maintenant vive Monet! Vive Rodin! (For ever Monet! For ever Rodin!) Hurrah!" had launched an era of true prosperity and sounded the knell on that terrible period of unpaid bills.

Thus by 1901, five gardeners were working in the garden which luxuriated in a deceptive simplicity, while another was employed solely to look after the pond which Monet had had dug several years earlier, and which he was about to have enlarged.

In the previous year, he had exhibited landscapes inspired by this water-garden at

Durand-Ruel's gallery. Now, in 1903, he was preparing for his first exhibition at the Bernheim brothers' gallery. This would forever change his relationship to money: his paintings would have a zero added to the price with remarkable regularity until by 1910 they were costing an average of 12,000 francs per canvas. The time was approaching when *Women in the Garden*, rejected for exhibition at the official Salon in 1867, would sell for 20,000 francs.

During this period, Monet's presence at Giverny attracted a lot of people, and this sleepy, peasant village found itself home to a colony of American artists. Some of them lived at the café-cum-grocery which had become the delightful Hotel Baudy. It was here that they drank straight liquor and played the piano or the banjo until late at night. Others rented or bought houses in which they led an active, and often sophisticated, social life. They held at-homes, garden parties, and soirées, at which they wore camellia buttonholes. The guest lists included many Americans living in Paris.

All the painters who asked for lessons and others who sought an invitation out of simple curiosity had to be politely but firmly turned away. All this led Monet to isolate himself even further.

The years slipped by, each using up its store of simple pleasures and complicated troubles, dominated by a very full calendar of wonderful meals. Between the ordinary days and the days on which there were

Below: two group photos of the family gathered for the picnics that were always held to celebrate the hunting season. Monet didn't hunt but he loved game.

guests, there were the Sunday family lunches, and the celebration lunches on June 6, Monet's saint's day, and November 14, Monet's birthday. Then, of course, there were the Christmas and New Year's lunches, in addition to the ceremonial picnics which were not to be missed for anything, especially the one held to celebrate the opening of the hunting season.

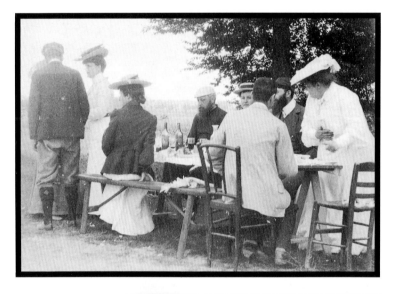

Pages 70-71: During the hunting season, the folding trestle table would be set up on the hillside in the shade of an apple tree.

Above: Claude
Monet, *Luncheon*,
c. 1873, Musée du
Louvre, Paris.

Opposite: Claude
Monet, *Luncheon
on the Grass*
(central fragment),
1865-1866. Paris,
Musée d'Orsay.

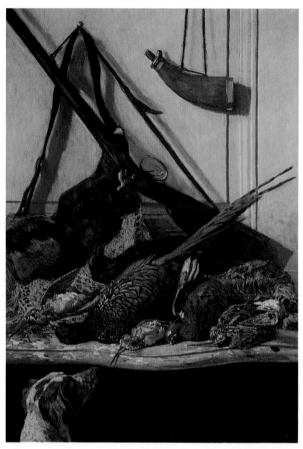

Above: Claude Monet, *Hunting Trophies*, 1862, Paris. Musée d'Orsay.

Marguerite reigned and tormented herself in the blue kitchen overlooking the garden. From mid-April, she could watch the flowering of two Japanese apple trees, which produced a wealth of pink-and-white blossom. She was surrounded by all her pans, pots, casseroles, and copper fish-kettles, her baking trays for méringues, her strings of molds, and the country stove for baking her apple tarts. There were strainers and sieves, pottery dishes – which she called stone dishes – for baking a red fruit pie, along with the weighing scales, the ancient ice cream maker, and the nutmeg grinder. She had an enormous amount of work, even when helped by first one, and later two, kitchen-maids.

Once the kitchen-garden vegetables had been delivered very early in the morning, she would prepare a hot first course for luncheon. Then there would be a meat or fish dish, sometimes both, a hot vegetable, a salad, and a different dessert every day, as well as cakes for teatime.

The evening meal began with soup – dinner without soup would have been inconceivable – and this was followed by an egg or cheese dish, such as individual soufflés served in ramekins. Then would come the main course, or *plat de résistance,* which might be poultry, a gratin dish or cold meat, plus a salad and cheese. No special dessert was made for dinner. Either dessert left over from lunch would be finished, or one of Marguerite's compotes would be served – cherries, plums, or peaches preserved in their own juice. No one could make them like Marguerite; she would serve them with a cookie or a piece of sponge cake.

Monet liked his chicory, green beans, and even chestnuts steamed. He also insisted on having his spinach cooked "in hardly any water" to preserve the flavor and color. He liked cèpes (wild mushrooms) in olive oil; according to the family, this was the only recipe which he could claim to have invented. He often demanded guinea-fowl, which could only be bought from Ledanois.

All this would have driven any household crazy. The worst moment of all was when an art dealer announced he was about to pay a call. According to season, the hunters in the family would be warned that the best game was required, or the best pike, for which Monet would have to pay dearly – even if he bought it from the gardener, who would have netted it from a boat in Monet's own pond. Or Sylvain might be sent out to buy turbot or the almost legendary monkfish.

The ceremony of selecting Florimond's tiniest vegetables would add to this disruption of the household, because everything had to be perfect for Messrs. Durand-Ruel or Bernheim, to say nothing of Thadée Natanson, in whose honor two ducks would be served, or Whistler, who was given pigeon stew. Theodore Butler (Suzanne's American husband who, after her tragic death in 1899, married Marthe) would be served with Lobster Newburg, prepared from the Delmonico's recipe. He was also treated to Welsh rarebit and the red cabbage which reminded him of Pennsylvania red cabbage. Each of the sons- and daughters-in-law brought their own customs and tastes with them.

To add to the difficulties, if the guest happened to be someone whom the boys judged to be boring, Alice or Blanche had to request picnic baskets for them. The boys were so used to their plant and insect collections that they would describe visitors whom they did not like in entomological terms.

It was not uncommon, after the Monets had had guests or taken a trip to Paris, for the cook to find herself presented with a new recipe which must be attempted, while following the instructions most closely. It is tantalizing to conjecture about what happened to the recipe for fillet of sole Marguéry, or to wonder how Marguerite could cook from another indecipherable recipe presented by Maupassant.

After one of Monet's trips to London, Marguerite had to learn to make Yorkshire Pudding as served at the Savoy Hotel. It is not known why Madame Renoir's famous *bouillabaisse* does not appear in the journals; perhaps some of the ingredients were unobtainable at Giverny.

On the other hand, three recipes provided by the Guitry family were included in the journals – Sacha's shoulder of pork, Lucien Guitry's lamb stew, and Charlotte Lysès's stuffed white onions. Charlotte Lysès was a very famous actress of the period; she was Sacha's first wife, and was adored by the whole family. Millet's recipe for bread rolls appears after Mallarmé's recipe for chanterelle mushrooms, Cézanne's salt cod soup, and lobster American-style from Drouant's. There are Foyot pork chops from the restaurant of the same name, oxtail stew from Marguéry's, Florentine fillets of sole from the Café de Paris, Julien's brill Dugléré-style, and of course upside down apple tart from the Tatin sisters.

It is easy to see why women who have cooked for the famous have made their names. Clemenceau had his Marie in the Rue Franklin, Dumas had his own Marie, and Degas his Zoé. Thus, in Monet's household, after Rita, Caroline, and Melanie, there could only be Marguerite.

As often happens when the household routine is of paramount importance, there was little difference between ordinary days

Opposite: Baked peaches fresh from the oven, one of the traditional Sunday desserts (recipe on page 166).

and those on which guests were invited. The menus may have been chosen a little more carefully to allow for the tastes of the visitors, but the table was set just as attractively for everyday. The tablecloths were always yellow and only two sets of tableware were ever used. These were the underglaze blue Creil earthenware of the pattern called Japon, with its stylized dark-blue cherry-trees and fans, and the white porcelain service with the wide yellow border and blue edging reserved for special days and important guests. The table centerpiece consisted of little bouquets of flowers from the garden or greenhouse, tiny honey-colored orchids and bee-orchids, wild flowers, or clematis floating in plain bowls. It had to look completely uncontrived.

Two cabinets from the Pays de Caux in Normandy displayed the family silver – soup tureens, tankards, chocolate pots, and coffee pots, while next to a pyramid of fruits and the decanters stood the big silver samovar for tea.

Dishes were served elegantly in the Monet household but were not given elaborate names or garnishes.

It is a matter of great regret that the everyday menus were never written down. If only Monet had taken a leaf from Whistler's book – it was Whistler's custom not only to write them down but also to decorate them with a little drawing, before autographing them with his famous Japanese-style butterfly monogram.

It was in this setting of chrome yellow furniture and walls, and among Monet's superb collection of Japanese prints, that the celebratory lunches took place. Such was the lunch held each year on November 14, Monet's birthday.

Before the event, the male members of the family would vie for the honor of killing the woodcock, or several if possible, for the occasion. But it was Jean-Pierre, the best shot, who became the official purveyor of the delicacy. Unlike other game, wood-cock does not spoil, and those who like it prefer it well-hung, though perhaps not to the point which Monet did. It was left to hang for 14 days in the cellar, then plucked and oven-roasted.

Paul, the butler, would present it at table, accompanied by a large slice of bread. Monet would remove the innards, spread them on the bread, and eat it. This was the

Above: On Christmas Day the famous truffled foie gras pâté ordered from Strasbourg was one of the delicacies served.

normal way to treat small feathered game, such as thrush with juniper berries, but in the case of woodcock the gizzard was generally first removed and discarded. For this birthday lunch, the woodcock had to be home-caught; on that day, game was not bought from the dealer.

Apart from the woodcock, two other dishes were customarily served, a large fish – pike or turbot – and a dessert, the *vert-vert*, that looked as good as it tasted. This was a cake, flavored with pistachio and frosted with glistening green fondant, as exotic as something out of an oriental fairytale. The rest of the meal varied according to the year and the inspiration of the moment.

In this household which had expe-rienced so many rituals and clearly marked seasons, the most magnificent meal, as for most families, was the Christmas lunch.

For once, they dined at midday. The dining-room was bedecked with simple garlands of leaves and flowers, and the best crystal and silverware were laid out on the best tablecloth with the yellow dishes. The bowls in the center of the table held clusters of white viburnum, Christmas roses and jasmine. The children would find at their places those little gray envelopes lined with rose madder, containing money from La Bonne (short for "La Bonne Maman" or grandmother) and Monet. Next to the napkins, there were mysterious little packets of sweets and small gifts – pins, medalions, and pocket watches. The large presents were waiting under the tree which had been installed in the mauve drawing-room.

For Christmas lunches, an old custom was revived, one which had survived from the days when a strict caste system ruled the farmyard. The goose had been placed at the bottom of the social scale and chicken was at the top, though only capons and fatted hens were deemed worthy to appear at a good table.

The menu began with eggs scrambled with truffles, or monkfish cooked American-style. Traditionally, Strasbourg truffled foie gras in pastry was served before the truffled, stuffed capons were presented on a bed of chestnuts and Périgord truffles, served with a chestnut purée. A light salad of lamb's lettuce would offset the heaviness of these dishes, fol-

Pages 80 – 87: The garden and house in mid-winter. Everyone was preparing to celebrate Christmas. By their places at the table, the children would find the famous "little packets" – small, pale-gray envelopes containing a sum of money – as well as mysterious little boxes of candies.

lowed by a Roquefort or Gorgonzola cheese. Finally, there came that moment which constituted the true magic of Christmas for the children. Paul would close the shutters and bring in the Christmas pudding, over which a generous measure of rum had been poured. He would strike a match and set light to the pudding, to the great joy of all present who would cry out in admiration. The crystal decanters containing wine and champagne would suddenly shine with greater brilliance.

To complete the festivities, homemade banana ice cream from the reliable old ice cream maker would make its appearance, looking like a sugarloaf. As usual, coffee would be served in the studio-drawing-room, followed by the brandies and liqueurs.

The next day's lunch at Marthe and Theodore Butler's was just as gargantuan, but they served the cheese after the dessert, American-style.

With time, as they married off, the family became rather scattered, but a celebration would soon bring them together again. Reunions around a well-stocked table or a lunch served outdoors strengthened the ties between them even further.

Thus, the first sunny days would find them packing picnic-hampers into their boats or cars, opening the picnicking season which was strung out throughout the year. There was the Mascaret picnic, the

Opposite and
above: Christmas
was the main
festival to which
Marguerite's cuisine
made a major
contribution in the
form of candies,
chocolates and
cakes. All these
good things were
accompanied by
large quantities of
Veuve Clicquot
champagne.

Côte de Gaillon Racetrack picnic, the Paris-Madrid Road Race picnic, and many others which had not been endowed with special names. The family would bring along a few close friends such as Pierre and Jean Sisley, Lucien Pissarro, Fernand Haundorf, the young Perry girls, and Germain Raingo, one of the few cousins admitted to this kind of outing. The rest were so indescribably chic and conventional that they couldn't possibly be taken along.

*I*n fact, once the good weather had come, one picnic followed another, worthy descendants of those very first lunches al fresco in the garden when Monet, Alice, and their eight children had just arrived, so many years before. The memories of them were a pleasant reminder of the first days spent at Giverny, when thousands of plans were being hatched in the excitement of having finally found a true home.

For numerous reasons, visitors to Monet's home were usually invited to a meal, but obviously most of the guests were more interested in Monet's painting and his ideas for a garden, than in a meal outdoors which could, in fact, have been eaten anywhere. It is surprising how many people love the countryside, but prefer to look at it through a drawing-room window, from a hotel terrace or through a car windshield.

There is a very big difference between strolling along the paths of the water garden or crossing the Japanese bridge, and venturing, basket in hand, into the forest to look for wild mushrooms. After such an excursion, one drops down on to a plaid blanket to lunch on the ground, throwing one's hat into the bushes and breathing in the damp air of the undergrowth, before returning to an automobile, which stands in a cloud of insolent mosquitoes and whose coughing engine refuses to start.

Alice loved the garden, the pond and the beauty of the countryside but no one ever saw her with pruning-shears or watering can in hand. She could be found with a cup of tea, working on something, or reading on the balcony and contemplating the garden below. On the other hand, she was the first to leap into the automobile for any sort of outing.

The hunting season was the time for a family migration, including all the cousins who had come to stay in neighboring houses. Some came from the Vendée, others from Cagnes or Rouen. All were experienced hunters, including the women. They would set off early in the morning, with beaters and hare-coursers, armed with shotguns and blunderbusses, and return exhausted at lunchtime, to be feted with the sacrosanct picnic which marked the opening of the season. Baskets and hampers of victuals had been packed into the automobiles, together with trestles and chairs. The folding table was set up on the hillside, under a spreading apple tree, where it awaited the heroes of the day.

Monet did not hunt but he adored game, especially partridge, and he was even fonder of woodcock. This did not stop him from often intoning, at the sight of the pâtés *en croute*, the wild rabbit and duck terrines, which were the traditional menu for that day: "Come eat, eat, let us eat this pigeon which will only be good if it is eaten hot." The luncheon, during which the hunters regaled the company with their usual exaggerations, ended with fruit tarts, fresh fruit and praise for the various bottles of cider and wine. This was one of the last such lunches of the year when the weather was good. Although July and August were frequently wet, September was usually a fine month at Giverny.

The family did a great deal of driving – the speed bug had bitten them – and even Monet would not for the world have missed the picnic held to watch the Paris-Madrid Rally go by in the Beauce plain. He was even more enthusiastic about the Côte de Gaillon Race. From then on, the nearest forests were abandoned in favor of others further afield from which they would bring back baskets full of cèpes. Anything was a good excuse for an excursion and a picnic. Monet would even let himself go, to the extent of singing, "Espoir charmant, Sylvain m'a dit, je t'aime." ("Delightful hope, Sylvain said to me, I love you," a popular

Pages 92-93: The yellow-bordered porcelain with the blue edging was only used for special occasions and for distinguished guests.

song.) Sylvain organized and led the expeditions to visit the Tatin sisters, to sample several of their famous apple tarts at La Mothe-Beuvron.

In the village of Giverny, truly good food was important to alot of people. At the inn, Madame Baudy would try to please her American guests by preparing Boston baked beans and stuffed spareribs, while all the young artists would sing the praises of squash and Philadelphia pepper pot which, so they said, had helped the troops of a general who was unknown in Giverny to win a battle no one had ever heard of. This fact did not stop them from forgetting their sorrows in a waltz or a cakewalk.

For the servants, the days were busy and very long. Like many domestics in their day, they had only the vaguest notions of leisure. In the noble tradition of families of grooms from the Sologne region, Sylvain would relax in the evenings by playing the hunting horn in the garden. Marguerite, instead of dreaming of some tranquil shore, would sit perched on her rocking-chair absorbed in a cookbook, such as *Pot-au-Feu* or *Luculle*.

In the meantime, in the mauve drawing-room, people would be reading old-fashioned, impracticable recipes. The next menu would be discussed while browsing through a catalog from the publisher Charpentier, or embroidering while sucking candies from Fouquet, bergamot oranges candied in honey, or violet bonbons from

Paris. The menu would certainly not be composed for its health-giving powers. In this household, it was inadvisable to admit to being indifferent to good food. Nothing could be more suspect; one would soon be taxed with philistinism, and be treated with a hint of condescension.

There would be few recipes here of the invalid beef-tea type, nor any of those Lenten menus, which were treated with what could be called Alice's bigotry. No one would think of dieting, although one might toy with the idea of a homeopathic remedy, such as the one prescribed by J. Prost-Lacuzon, and prepared by the famous Georges Weber pharmacy in the Rue des Capucines for Alice. It left no doubt as to her preoccupations : "Arsenicum, Sulphur, Calc. carb. (Calcarea Carbonica), Iodium, to be taken in alternate weeks. Follow a diet, increase the amount of exercise, lead a very active life, etc..."

At the slightest indisposition, one could rush to consult the book of medicinal remedies. This would be followed by a raid on Florimond's kitchen-garden, for a few leaves of melissa, alpine mint, or even borage to soothe coughing on cold nights, although tea made from violet flowers had a more delicate flavor.

This book of medicinal remedies – which advised on the treatment of chlorosis in young girls, fevers of all kinds, and excessive eating – contained a chapter on mental illnesses, and misanthropy in particular, which was to be combatted by taking five different preparations in 12th and 13th dilutions.

A day had to be arranged on which to invite those cousins whom one wouldn't dare take on a picnic because they were so elegant and starchy, and who seemed to treat the Monets like friendly natives. Aunt Cécile Rémy, whose majesty appeared as though it would crush the whole garden, was the very image of Aunt Marguerite Le Moyne. In fact, all the aunts and cousins wanted to see for themselves what a successful painter looked like, but it is never much fun for those who are being stared at like animals at the zoo. Of course, the guests were delighted: Monsieur Monet was famous.

In the very small room, the children spoke more openly of Ernest Hoschedé, whose image still floated before them, as they leafed through copies of *Art et La Mode*, which he had founded and in which Stéphane Mallarmé had published his "White Waterlily."

Yet the atmosphere was not gloomy in the mauve drawing-room –which resembled an aviary most of the time. Monet had been quite right to remove his studio to the other end of the garden and allow no one inside without his permission. Only Alice was admitted. She would sit there embroidering, sewing, and talking about painting to Monet. Later, Blanche took her place.

In that little mauve drawing-room one could admit to liking Maxime du Camp, not understanding Ibsen, and detesting Zola or Barrès. Russian novels and the stories of Turgenev were devoured enthusiastically, as were the poems of Mallarmé, his wonderful letters, and his stories, which were just as interesting. There was much discussion of the latest news of the fire at the Opéra-Comique, and of La Tarasque who was going north from the Rhone Valley to settle in Paris.

Monet traveled almost every year, and wrote home every day. After much persuasion from his family, in his letters from London he described in greater detail than usual the grand occasions he attended, even describing such aspects as the dresses, for the benefit of his daughters-in-law who would have loved to have joined him.

John Singer Sargent usually organized Monet's trips, whisking him through a whirlwind of dinners in town. He introduced Monet to curators, collectors, Princess Louise and the London world of art and politics. He even took him to view the grandiose spectacle of Queen Victoria's funeral, which he watched from the window of a friend's house. This was the day on which Monet made the acquaintance of Henry James. Reynaldo Hahn gives us a glimpse of this London which was more exciting than Paris. There was, for instance,

the Bath-Club in Dover Street where half of Europe took a dip before going to immerse themselves in the calmer waters of Carlsbad. To someone living in the country, the London chronicles and the trips to Paris, like visits from friends, were indispensable for preventing the most fatal intellectual lethargy.

Of course, matters were not always so simple, especially when Monet, who was always courteous toward his guests, made a scene or declined one of the exciting invitations with which he was continually bombarded – for example, staying with the Potter-Palmers in Chicago or at the Palazzo Barbaro with Mary Hunter, visiting with Mrs. Sargent Curtis, or traveling to Japan or even India.

Below: Monet was fond of chestnuts, but he liked them steamed. They were served in a variety of dishes.

Birds of Passage

"*Run away to a village to make it*
the center of the world."

JULES RENARD, *DIARY*

Above: Claude Monet, *The Cakes (Les Galettes)*, 1882, private collection, Paris.

Monet, who was so demanding, who had his work and adored comfort and good food, also loved nature to a degree rarely found in a town-dweller. In him, qualities that would in most people be in conflict were reconciled. He was simultaneously a bourgeois and a country-man, a bon viveur and an ascetic.

For Alice, life was not so simple, and this fundamental difference between the two of them was noticeable. Although she shared all of Monet's interests, he would retreat into his work totally absorbed,

Opposite: Tea was served in the garden whenever the weather permitted. Monet liked strong tea, which came from the Kardomah shop.

leaving her with a prospect of emptiness before her. This was especially the case on those long winter days he often chose for his painting campaigns, and whole months would go by when he would not hold a proper conversation with anyone at all. Yet Alice was in her element when surrounded by friends. For her, the regular trips to Paris were almost certainly as vital as the migrations of those birds of passage who landed in the garden.

Vernon, the neighboring town where the family shopped, had caught up with the

97

times, and it was now possible to buy numerous delicacies there: Ceylon, Darjeeling or China teas, Italian cheeses from Paris, as well as clothing, candies from Fouquet, visiting cards, leather, chintz, and cretonne for the day-beds in the studios.

When the Monets went to Paris on shopping trips, or to meet a dealer, organize an exhibition, dine with friends, or see a show, they would either take the train to the Saint-Lazare railroad station, or go by automobile. Sylvain, who was frightened of driving in town, would drop them at the Porte de Saint-Cloud. They would stay at the Hotel Terminus, which served as the headquarters for the whole family, especially Butler and Marthe, and later Jim and Lily, Butler's children. Remaining on the right bank of the Seine, they would hurry to the great buildings designed by Hausmann in which the art galleries had taken root. Here the Monets' passions for art and for good food could both be indulged with ease.

For their restaurants, they would actually visit relatively few arrondissements. They would wander between the Seine and what was then called the Boulevard, between Saint-Augustin and the Alexander III Bridge, from the Place de l'Europe to the Tuileries gardens, between the Passage du Havre, the Passage Choiseul and the Passage des Panoramas, between Marigny and the Faubourg Saint-Denis.

Their trips were timed to coincide with the Salons and the Universal Exhibitions. Although their sons frequented the races at the Vélodrome, and visited the shows at the Palais de l'Automobile and the botanical gardens, they themselves would frequent a more literary side of Paris. Their most daring excursions were to visit the theaters. They often attended opening nights of plays, especially those of their good friend, Mirbeau. They also went to see their actor friends, such as Coquelin in *Le Bourgeois Gentilhomme*, Lucien Guitry in *Chantecler*, Eve Lavallière at the Théâtre des Variétés, and Mademoiselle Desprès at the Théâtre Antoine in *Poil de Carotte*. Naturally, they were familiar with the almost inexhaustible list of music-halls. At about this time, Paris was listening to the sayings of Alphonse Allias, Courteline's jokes, Tristan Bernard's wit, and the still incomprehensible ideas of Alfred Jarry.

They listened to Rose Caron, a great interpreter of Wagner's music, and to Chaliapine in *Boris Godunov* and went to the Folies Bergères to watch Loïe Fuller (presented by the sculptor, Rodin) performing her snake-dance. Then there were the Javanese dancers, and those from the Cambodian Ballet Royal. They heralded the arrival of the Ballets Russes, directed by Diaghilev, that tornado of a man, with scenery by Bakst and the scandalous *L'Après-midi d'un Faune* danced by Nijinsky. Most unexpected was Alice's taste for wrestling matches which were extremely violent.

The pace was fast: one show a day, a different restaurant each evening or dinner with friends. Clearly, even if one tried to avoid excessive noise and bustle, Paris was not to be visited with impunity.

Monet had instituted their Friday Dîner Drouant, and on the first Thursdays of the month, Mallarmé, Georges de Bellio, Caillebotte and Renoir would meet at the Café Riche. They had set up many dinners and

Above: June, 1921. Monet standing with Clemenceau and Lily on the Japanese bridge.

With regard to the restaurants patronized by the Monets, those untypical times were long past when Monet had preferred a simple stew, eating in places frequented by emaciated young men wearing voluminous greatcoats, who seemed to live on a diet of milk and aphorisms. It was a long time since the art critic Geffroy and

meetings of one group or another that it was impossible to keep up the pace.

The name has been lost of the restaurant at which Monet and Antonin Proust dined after their seconds had dissuaded them from fighting a duel. The custom of the day was to go to Ledoyen after having fought bravely in the Bois de Boulogne; this had also been the headquarters of Ernest Hoschedé after his visits to the Salons. In the 1900's, Monet and Alice would dine at Prunier's, Julien's, the Café de Paris, the Café Anglais, or Marguéry's, always choosing dishes that were not served at Giverny.

At Drouant, they would dine with Eugène Carrière, Rodin, Ajalbert, Lucien Descaves, Maurice Joyant, Rosny, Clemenceau, and Edmond de Goncourt. After eating their woodcock Drouant-style, or brill in red wine, it was the custom to order Josette pears which absolutely had to be accompanied by an Haut-Brion wine reserved for the occasion by Drouant himself. Goncourt would wax lyrical at these Friday dinners, and nostagically recall the crayfish butter which had been invented in his native Lorraine (lost to France in the Franco-Prussian war, but restored to her in 1918).

All these famous personalities who used to meet in Paris would hurry down to Giverny at the first opportunity, hardly waiting to be asked. Naturally, they wanted to come in the summer to see the gardens and Alice was kept busy organizing this wave of visitors. She had to make endless arrangements and deal with every sort of interruption. It was very difficult, even unthinkable, not to accede to the requests of admirers who had been recommended by a dealer or a friend. When Monet was engrossed in his work, it meant

he had to stop and tidy his studio, causing a complete break in that demanding schedule of creativity in its pure state. It also meant taking the risk of displeasing someone who might become a collector.

Yet Alice enjoyed having guests, especially as Monet's friends were never boring or colorless. Of course, there were a few fashionable people who were rather too gossipy and who would talk alot of nonsense just to make themselves sound amusing; the wife of a certain painter had to be tolerated despite the stories she was capable of inventing. But that sort of person was soon overwhelmed by all the others.

Curiously, Monet, who had always tried to keep his prices high, even in his most difficult times, and had refused to allow any dealer exclusive rights, managed to maintain a friendship based on a business relationship, with both the Bernheim brothers and with Durand-Ruel. However, things did not always go well, especially as this house was not exactly full of people noted for their diplomacy.

Alice, who had retained a talent for spending the housekeeping money agreeably, left over from the days when she lived in splendor, knew better than anyone how important it was to treat the dealers properly.

Alice received her guests in a house smothered under young vines and roses, surrounded by a garden in which the

seasons appeared as a succession of different beautifully-controlled harmonies. The color scheme changed from crimson, softened by banks of pink or white, to the bronze tide of late August, giving way to all the blues and mauves of the fall.

This walled universe increased the impression of isolation and serenity, and few would have dared to arrive unannounced to disturb Monet. Sacha Guitry, who thought this rule did not apply to him, found himself forced to go on his way.

Friends from Paris were joined by those from London and Venice, as well as Americans, mainly from the east coast and Chicago. The only local resident who visited was the Abbé Toussaint, converted to cosmopolitanism by the force of events.

Above: Monet and his friend, the horticulturist Georges Truffaut, examining the Japanese peonies in the garden at Giverny.

Otherwise they came from all over, taking the train at the Saint-Lazare station for Vernon, where a car had been ordered to meet them. A few stalwarts preferred to walk from there. The most fashionable people came by boat down the Seine; these included Caillebotte, Mirbeau, the Depeaux, the Helleus, the Johnstons, and many others. They abandoned their hotels, houses, and overdecorated apartments to relax in this rural setting. Here, they would lunch in very simple, though ultra-modern surroundings, accentuated here and there by a piece of Delft pottery or an Arita vase, or by the blue and coppery sheen of an Imari vase, or even a discreet East India Company epergne, one of the rare pieces of "famille rose" porcelain to have escaped the horrors of the forced public auctions at Rottenbourg.

It was customary for guests to arrive in the late morning to lunch at 11:30, after viewing the latest paintings in the studio and paying a short visit to the greenhouses. Conversation became animated between the time when the coffee was served in the drawing-room and teatime. Tea was served under the lime-trees, on the balcony or near the pond. Sometimes people would climb the stairs to look at Monet's private collection of paintings by Cézanne, Renoir, Pissarro, Degas, Morisot, Manet, Signac, Corot, and Delacroix. The display never included all the paintings and would frequently be changed.

At teatime, Paul would bring in the boiling water, and Alice, or later Blanche, would dole out teaspoons of the precious tea-leaves from Kardomah; scones, chestnut cookies, or cinnamon toast would be served.

Everyone knew how strictly Monet kept to his timetable. He hated visitors to use their own transportation because they would always be late, or get lost on the way, or have one, two or even three breakdowns. Marguerite once confided that one day she thought he would sit down at table without waiting for the guests, he was so annoyed at seeing his daily schedule disrupted.

So many people came here that it is impossible to list them all. Painter friends,

such as Renoir, Sisley, Pissarro, and Cézanne, used to visit during the early, difficult days. Later, they were joined by other artists, such as Eugène Carrière, Paul Helleu, and John Singer Sargent. There were even a few artists from Giverny's American colony such as Lilla Cabot Perry, Theodore Robinson, and obviously, Theodore Earl Butler, who had become one of the family through marriage. The Monets were very close friends with the Caillebottes, who had helped them at those very critical periods when they had no money, as well as with Berthe Morisot and Degas. A more distant relationship developed later with the American Impressionist, Mary Cassatt and even later with Vuillard, K.X. Roussel and Pierre Bonnard. Even Matisse paid them one or two visits.

The numerous artists interested in Monet's work were joined by writers such as Stéphane Mallarmé or Paul Valéry as well as Georges Clemenceau, who understood the progress of the water-lily paintings very well and wrote about them in his books. Those who were most highly regarded by Monet and Alice were probably Mallarmé, Rodin, Mirbeau, Clemenceau, Gustave Geffroy, and certainly Durand-Ruel.

The dealer Maurice Joyant announced his visit with Isaac de Camondo to acquire *Cathedrals*, while Lucien Guitry wanted to bring Anatole France, which greatly pleased Monet. The Bernheims sent the Prince de Wagram, who drove so fast that they did not want to come down with him in his automobile.

Sacha Guitry and Charlotte Lysès were frequent visitors to Giverny as was Mary Hunter, a friend of Sargent. Fasquelle, Gallimard, and Charpentier represented the world of publishing. Other welcome guests included Henry Farman, a British aviator who painted in his spare time, and the eccentric Whistler. Whistler would often receive his own guests in a sort of kimono; he would cook the meal himself and had no hesitation in coloring the food he served his guests to match his underglaze blue dinner service.

Japanese influence, which was all the rage in the west, was to be found everywhere. Commodore Perry, who had first discovered Japan for the west, had a great-nephew living in Giverny.

There were Japanese woodcuts on the walls, Japanese pottery and vases, oiled paper sunshades, little wooden houses, and a white porcelain figure of a sleeping cat, which was left on the sofa of the third studio to symbolize the fact that all cats were forbidden entry because they dug up the flowerbeds. There were all the books of woodcuts or translated stories presented as gifts by friends, not to mention the Japanese lily bulbs, so rare in France, which were sent to Giverny from Japan. There were also items which were Japanese-inspired, like the Creil china, or the habit of embroidering initials or first names in a vertical arrangement. All this was, however, a far cry from the erudite bric-a-brac to be found at Edmond de Goncourt's home, which was exhibited in the annex to the Universal Exhibition. Anything unusual was dubbed "Japanese."

It is strange to find no trace of a special menu for the Japanese guests. The Kuroki family were among the first Japanese to visit Monet's house and buy paintings. Madame Kuroki was a close friend of Blanche; her grandmother, the Marchioness Matsukata, had been a member of the the immediate entourage of the Empress.

Naturally, in their shuttling back and forth between Tokyo, Marseilles and Paris, the Kurokis had had much opportunity to become Westernized. They did so just enough to be able to tolerate the unesthetic jumble of Western tastes, the food served ungarnished and the decorations displayed in such suffocating profusion. Monet and Alice knew that the Japanese of every era have liked sobriety, purity of line, and monochrome color schemes. At Giverny, the Japanese were served with the white and yellow dinner service with the blue edging, because the blue service, which was a French imitation of Japanese pottery, might have appeared to be some sort of practical joke by the manufacturer.

Other Japanese visitors, Monsieur Bing, Monsieur Hayashi and Monsieur Kazunori Ishibashi, who were all esthetes, were reassured by the little Japanese inscription in blue, painted on a flower-block, which congratulated Monet on behalf of all Japan for having been one of the first painters in the West to have abandoned perspective. They also admired the Japanese pottery on the mantelpiece which was painted with a design of bats. What with these visitors, as well as such people as Bernard Berenson, Sir William Rothenstein, and a certain Mr. Calder (an artist himself and father of the sculptor Alexander Calder), Giverny could have easily been mistaken for a suburb of Boston or Yokohama!

The visitors represented the widest spectrum of political opinion. There were, for instance, both admirers and detractors of Victor Hugo. But this was no problem. Nor were the menus or the tastes and opinions of the guests. The real challenge of these luncheons was to provide a suitable means of transporting the guests – some of whom preferred a horse and carriage, while others were addicted to speed.

Then there were the unpredictable moods of Degas. He was perfectly capable of making one die of laughter at his aphorisms, but only if everyone was in step with him. One couldn't invite him with Paul Helleu, whom he had dubbed "the steam Watteau."

Lunches at Giverny posed many other problems. Too many very different people encountered each other there. The times were just too loaded with explosives. There was the day, for example, when Rodin found Cézanne on his knees before him in the garden thanking him for having shaken his hand. Cézanne, with his temperamental and hypersensitive nature, was prone to bizarre, unpredictable behavior.

With Rodin there were innumerable subjects to avoid, such as his complicated love affairs which were public knowledge. Yet Rodin sent Giverny one of the most beautiful dancers ever, Isadora Duncan, who captivated the sons of the family. For Monet, Isadora danced as Nijinsky had danced for Rodin, and Marguerite Namara from the Chicago Opera played the piano in Monet's large studio known as the Waterlily Studio.

Clemenceau remained a close family friend, even though his involvement in the 1892 Panama Canal Company scandal put him in an extremely delicate position.

At the time, Clemenceau had become involved in a duel which made him a figure of fun. In the election the following year, Clemenceau was defeated. (Nine years later, however, he was reelected, eventually to become Prime Minister once more.)

Life at Giverny for Monet included reading the works of Paul Valéry, plucking a faded iris head, and receiving the whole

world or at least a third of it. It was chatting to Delphine, who had come to deliver the starched linen, running off to London to grumble at the parliament building which was so impossible to paint, and smoking those dreadful Caporal Rose cigarettes to the last days of his life.

The assassination of Archduke Ferdinand plunged the whole world into war. At Giverny, as elsewhere, life became sad, complicated and much altered. Yet nothing totally interrupted the established rituals. There were the lunches with the Goncourt academicians in the Large Studio; the lunch with Clemenceau on November 14, 1918, in honor of Monet's birthday, three days after the Armistice; and the last great post-war lunches with the Kurokis.

Monet died in 1926 and Blanche, who had replaced her mother as mistress of the household after 1911, continued against all

Above: The Japanese bridge on a misty day.

Pages 106-107: Monet treated champagne like any other white wine and decanted it into a carafe for serving.

odds. Truly, when a Hoschedé-Monet was involved, there was no question of sinking into the habit of one-course meals and processed food .

Many years later, in September 1940, when the established order was once again upset, Blanche wrote to Count Metternich asking him to protect the house. An official notice was pinned to the door, stating, "This is Monet's house. Forbidden to the forces of occupation." Blanche could stop tormenting herself.

The house may have been protected but it was nonetheless deserted. And Blanche was almost alone in knowing that the revels of Giverny had truly come to an end on that day in June 1940, when the red truck of a traveling salesman took the last servants away.

It was done, Marguerite had handed in her apron.

THE RECIPES

A recipe from the
Café de Paris for
Florentine filets of
sole (see page 161).

Soups

Leek and Potato Soup

Soupe aux poireaux et pommes de terre

Serves 4

½ cup unsalted butter
5 or 6 large leeks, white parts only, cut into ½ inch slices
1 teaspoon salt
4 large potatoes, sliced

Heat ¼ cup of the butter in a pan and sauté the leeks. While they are cooking, heat 1 quart water with the salt to just below a boil . Add the water to the leeks, all at once. Cover the pan, reduce the heat and simmer for 45 minutes. Add the sliced potato, cover, and continue cooking for 20 minutes. Add the rest of the butter before serving.

Cream of Sorrel Soup

Potage Germiny

Serves 4

¼ cup unsalted butter
8 cups (1 pound) sorrel, washed and trimmed
5 cups Clear Broth (recipe on page 112) or consommé
2 egg yolks, beaten
4 slices French bread, about ½ inch thick

Melt 1 tablespoon of the butter in a saucepan over low heat. Add the sorrel and stir until it wilts. Pass the sorrel through a sieve, reserving the liquid.

Heat the broth or consommé with the sorrel liquid in a covered saucepan over low heat. When it is just below boiling point, remove from the heat and pour off 1 cup of the broth. Leave this to cool for a few minutes. Stir the beaten egg yolks into the reserved liquid. Pour this back into the broth, stirring constantly, and continue cooking until the liquid starts to thicken. Do not let it boil or it will curdle. When it thickens remove it from the heat but keep it warm.

Melt the rest of the butter in a skillet and sauté the slices of French bread on both sides until golden-brown. Place each one in a warmed, shallow soup bowl. Reheat the sorrel soup, stirring constantly, and when it is hot pour it over the slices of bread in the bowls.

Mixed Vegetable Soup

Potage Fontange

Serves 4

2 cups dried green or yellow peas
⅔ cup unsalted butter, softened
1 onion, thinly sliced
2 leeks, white parts only, sliced
2 cups (¼ pound) sorrel, trimmed and shredded
1 head of iceberg lettuce, trimmed and shredded
3 sprigs chervil , finely chopped
2 medium-size potatoes, peeled and cut in half
6 cups Rich Broth (recipe on page 113) or water
½ teaspoon salt
½ teaspoon pepper
2 egg yolks
1 cup heavy cream or crème fraîche
8 slices thinly sliced bread

Soak the dried peas in water for 2 hours, then drain. Melt 2 tablespoons of the butter in a pot. Add the onion, leeks, sorrel, lettuce, and chervil. Cook over low heat, stirring with a wooden spoon, until the vegetables are well-coated; do not let them brown. Add the dried peas and potatoes, then the Rich Broth or water. Season with the salt and pepper and bring to a boil. Cover and simmer over very low heat for at least 2 hours. Strain and reheat for a few minutes, stirring constantly.

Beat the rest of the butter into a smooth cream, then beat in the egg yolks and cream or crème fraîche. Pour this mixture into a soup tureen and pour the boiling hot soup over it. Serve with the thinly sliced bread.

Opposite: Soup was served at every
evening meal in Monet's house.
This is garlic soup (recipe on page 113).

111

Cream of Turnip Soup

Potage à la Dauphine

Serves 4

8 small, young white turnips (about 1 ¼ pounds)
¼ cup unsalted butter
2 cups light cream, half-and-half, or ⅓ cup unsalted butter
Salt and pepper

Scrape and wash the turnips well and put them in a pot with 1 ½ quarts water and the ¼ cup butter. Bring to a boil, then cover and simmer over low heat for about 30 minutes or until the turnips crush easily under a fork.

Remove the pot from the heat, and strain the contents, reserving the liquid. Purée the turnips. Return the turnips and reserved liquid to the pot and put it back on the heat. While the liquid is reheating, add the cream or the extra butter, cutting it into small pieces. Stir until the mixture is smooth and the butter, if used, has melted; do not let it boil. Season to taste. Serve hot.

Herb Soup

Soupe aux herbes

Serves 6

2 cups (¼ pound) sorrel, finely chopped
2 cups (¼ pound) fresh chervil, finely chopped
1 small head of iceberg or Boston lettuce, finely chopped
¼ cup unsalted butter
1 teaspoon coarse salt
1/8 teaspoon black pepper
½ cup rice

Melt half the butter in a flameproof casserole and add the herbs, lettuce, salt and pepper. Cook for five minutes, then add 6 cups hot water and partially cover. Simmer for 15 minutes. Rinse the rice and add it to the pot. Stir it well into the greens and cook over low heat for 30 minutes. Stir the mixture well before serving, and pour it into a warmed soup-tureen. Cut the rest of the butter into small pieces and add the pieces of butter to the soup before serving.

To Make A Good Clear Broth

Pour faire un bon consommé

Makes 4 quarts

Carcasses and giblets of 2 boiling chickens
6 carrots
4 small turnips
2 large leeks, trimmed and split lengthwise
1 celery stalk
1 large onion
2 cloves
1 sprig thyme
1 bayleaf
2 sprigs parsley
2 egg whites, well beaten

Pour 5 quarts water into a soup kettle. Add the carcasses and giblets and bring to a boil over moderate heat. Skim the surface until it is clear.

Tie the cloves, thyme, bayleaf, and parsley together in a piece of cheesecloth to make a bouquet garni. Add the carrots, turnips, leeks, celery and onion and the bouquet garni. Cover and simmer for 3 hours, skimming from time to time. Strain the broth.

If you want a very clear consommé you must clarify it. Let it cool completely, then degrease it by passing a paper towel over the surface.

Return the broth to the heat and when it is hot but not yet boiling, add the beaten egg whites. Stir very slowly until the liquid boils, then strain it through cheesecloth.

To Make A Rich Broth

Pour faire un bouillon gras

Makes 10 cups

3 pounds beef chuck or other inexpensive cut of meat
1 beef marrow bone
3 medium-size carrots
2 small turnips or 1 large turnip
1 onion
1 large leek, trimmed
2 sprigs parsley
1 sprig thyme
3 celery leaves
2 cloves

Pour 3 quarts water into a large soup kettle. Add the pieces of beef and the bone and bring to a boil, uncovered. Boil, partially covered, for 1 hour over medium heat, skimming occasionally. Tie the parsley, thyme, celery leaves, and cloves together in a piece of cheesecloth to make a bouquet garni. Add the vegetables and the aromatics tied in the cheesecloth and bring the liquid back to the boil. Reduce the heat and simmer, covered, for three hours. Strain the liquid. For a lighter, clearer broth, strain the liquid through cheesecloth.

Garlic Soup

Soupe à l'ail

Serves 6

12 garlic cloves, peeled
salt and pepper
6 eggs
⅓ cup unsalted butter
2 cups croutons
⅔ cup parsley, finely chopped

Put the garlic cloves into a pot and add 6 cups water. Bring to a boil and cook until the garlic is soft, about 15 minutes. Remove the garlic cloves and crush them to a smooth paste. Return this to the liquid, remove the pot from the heat and let it cool slightly.

Melt all but 2 tablespoons of the butter in a skillet and sauté the croutons, turning them constantly until they are evenly browned. Put them into a warmed soup tureen.

Break the eggs into a mixing bowl. Add 1 cup of the garlic liquid, beating well to prevent curdling.

Pour the egg mixture back into the pot, stirring constantly. Add the remaining 2 tablespoons of butter. Reheat the liquid but do not let it boil or it will curdle. Pour the hot soup over the croutons. Sprinkle with the chopped parsley and serve.

Cabbage Soup with Cheese

Garbure

This dish was made on the day a pot-au-feu stew was served. The cabbage can be replaced with a purée of vegetables from the stew, or other vegetables can be used. It is to be served as an accompaniment to a consommé or broth.

Serves 6

1 green cabbage
6−8 slices day-old bread
4 cups grated Cheddar cheese
4 cups broth

Trim the cabbage and pull the leaves apart. Blanch it in rapidly boiling water for 10 minutes, then drain it. Have another pot of boiling water ready and add the cabbage leaves to it. Cook them, covered, over low heat for 15 minutes. Drain and shred the leaves.

Preheat the oven to 400°. Grease an earthenware baking dish about 3 inches deep and arrange the slices of bread to cover the bottom. Arrange a layer of cabbage over the bread, then sprinkle with grated cheese. Cover the cheese with another layer of cabbage, then another layer of cheese. Continue layering until all the cabbage is used, ending with a layer of grated cheese.

Pour the broth over the mixture. Bake about 15 minutes or until the cheese is melted and golden. Serve directly from the baking dish, pouring soup or extra broth over each serving.

Eggs

Savory Egg Custard with Tomato Sauce

Oeufs renversés à la tomate

Serves 8

4 cups milk
¼ teaspoon salt
8 eggs
1 cup Gruyère cheese, grated
½ teaspoon pepper

Tomato Sauce

12 ripe tomatoes, peeled
2 sprigs thyme
1 bayleaf
½ teaspoon pepper
½ teaspoon salt
1 small slice ham, cut into julienne strips (optional)
2 tablespoons unsalted butter, cut into pieces

Heat the milk with the salt. When it comes to a boil, remove it from the heat but keep it warm.

Preheat the oven to 300°. Grease a large straight-sided mold, such as a Charlotte mold. Beat the eggs, as for an omelet. Continue beating while adding the warm milk, one tablespoon at a time, until the eggs are warmed, after about 6 tablespoons. Then add all the remaining milk, and the cheese. Stir and pour the mixture into the mold. Place it in a baking dish filled with enough water to come halfway up the sides of the mold. Bake for at least 30 minutes, or until the tip of a knife inserted into the center comes out clean. Remove from the oven and let it cool for at least 5 minutes before turning out onto a warmed platter.

While the custard is cooking, make the tomato sauce. Cut the tomatoes into quarters and press them lightly to extract excess juice and the seeds. Put the tomato pulp into a pan with the thyme and bayleaf. Add the salt and pepper. Bring to a boil, reduce the heat and simmer for at least 20 minutes or until it turns into a thick purée. Strain

Opposite: Scrambled eggs with truffles were traditionally served at Christmas (recipe for scrambled eggs on page 116).

the liquid and add the ham, if desired. Keep warm in a bain-marie until the eggs are ready. Just before serving, remove the sauce from the bain-marie (water bath) and stir in the butter, a piece at a time, until the mixture is smooth. Pour the sauce over the egg custard.

Poached Eggs au Gratin

Oeufs pochés à la lyonnaise

Serves 8

¼ cup vinegar
8 eggs
12 small white onions, minced
1 tablespoon unsalted butter
2 tablespoons flour
1 cup milk
1 cup Clear Broth (recipe on page 112)
½ teaspoon salt
½ teaspoon pepper
2 tablespoons grated Gruyère cheese

Pour 2 cups boiling water into a large skillet and add the vinegar. Break each egg individually and slide it into the boiling liquid, to poach it. Cover the skillet and cook for about 6 minutes, or until all the eggs are all poached. Remove each with a spatula and drain them on paper towels.

Put the onions into a saucepan with ½ cup boiling water and bring to a boil. Cook for 5 minutes, uncovered, or until slightly softened. Melt the butter in a saucepan and add the onions. Cook them gently for 5 to 10 minutes, or until they are just beginning to color. Stir in the flour, milk, and Clear Broth; cook, stirring constantly, until you have a thick white sauce. Season to taste with the salt and pepper.

Preheat the broiler. Grease a large shallow baking dish and pour half the sauce into it. Arrange the poached eggs on the sauce and pour the rest of the sauce over them. Sprinkle with the grated cheese. Place the dish under the broiler and broil on very high heat until the cheese browns and bubbles.

Stuffed Eggs

Oeufs berrichons

Serves 4

4 hardboiled eggs
2–3 sprigs parsley, chopped
1 small onion, minced
1 garlic clove, minced
¼ teaspoon salt
¼ teaspoon pepper
3 tablespoons heavy cream or crème fraîche

Slice the eggs in half lengthwise and remove the yolks. Mash the yolks and combine them with the parsley, onion, garlic, salt and pepper. Stir in the cream or crème fraîche. Fill the whites with the mixture.

Preheat the oven to 300°. Lightly grease a baking dish. Arrange the eggs in the dish. Bake the mixture for about 20 minutes or until the tops are just colored.

Eggs Orsini

Oeufs Orsini

This very easy dish is always successful, but it cannot be kept waiting when ready.

Serves 6

6 eggs
¼ teaspoon salt
¼ teaspoon pepper
2 tablespoons grated cheese
¼ cup unsalted butter, cut into small pieces

Break each egg separately, pouring the whites into a bowl but leaving the yolks in the shells. Try to remove the threads from the yolks, but do not break the yolks. Prop the shells up with paper towels or a cloth to keep the yolks from spilling out.

Add the salt to the whites and beat them until stiff. They should be stiff enough to support the weight of a teaspoon without it sinking in.

Preheat the oven to 300°. Grease an ovenproof dish and pour the whites into it all at once. Smooth the surface with a wooden spoon. Use the spoon handle to make six fairly deep cavities in the whites, evenly spaced and as far apart as possible. Slip one egg yolk into each cavity and sprinkle with pepper. Sprinkle the whole dish with the cheese and dot it with the butter.

Place the dish on the floor of the oven. Bake for 20–30 minutes or until the yolks are set. Serve the dish immediately.

Scrambled Eggs

Oeufs brouillés

Monet liked his eggs scrambled with wild mushrooms, such as morels, chanterelles or oyster mushrooms.

Serves 4

1 cup croutons
8 eggs
½ teaspoon salt
½ teaspoon pepper
½ cup unsalted butter, cubed
2 tablespoons minced chives, or 2 tablespoons minced truffles, or ½ cup chanterelle mushrooms, sautéed in unsalted butter for about 10 minutes (optional)

Divide the croutons between four warmed plates. Bring the water to a boil in a bain-marie (water bath) or double boiler. Break the eggs into a bowl, and carefully remove the threads of the whites without mixing the eggs too much. Add the salt and beat lightly, as for an omelet. The mixture must not foam.

Pour the eggs into a saucepan placed in the bain-marie or double boiler. Beat them well for 2 minutes, then add the pepper and continue beating until the mixture begins to thicken. Now add the cubes of butter, beating constantly after each addition. When the eggs are on the point of setting, add chives, truffles or chanterelle mushrooms if desired. As soon as the mixture becomes grainy, remove the saucepan from the heat and pour the contents over the croutons on the plates.

Opposite: Monet was very fond of wild mushrooms, which were often added to scrambled eggs.

Sauces

Tomato Sauce
Sauce à la tomate
Makes 1 ½ cups

½ cup unsalted butter
2 tablespoons flour
2 cups milk, scalded
¼ teaspoon salt
¼ teaspoon pepper
2 tablespoons tomato paste

Place the butter and flour in a saucepan and stir them into a smooth paste over low heat. Remove from the heat and gradually add the scalded milk, stirring constantly to prevent lumps from forming. Season with salt and pepper. Return the pan to the heat and continue to cook over low heat , stirring constantly, until the liquid boils. Stir in the tomato paste, and serve hot.

Béarnaise Sauce
Sauce béarnaise
Makes 1 cup

1 sprig thyme
2 sprigs parsley
2 sprigs tarragon
2 sprigs chervil
½ cup white vinegar
2 shallots, minced
3 egg yolks
½ cup unsalted butter, softened
¼ teaspoon salt
¼ teaspoon pepper

Tie the thyme, parsley and 1 sprig each of the tarragon and chervil into a piece of cheesecloth, to make a bouquet garni. Finely chop the remaining sprigs of tarragon and chervil. Pour the vinegar into a small saucepan and add the shallots and bouquet garni. Bring the liquid to a boil, then lower the heat and reduce the liquid for about 30 minutes over a low heat, until it is syrupy. Remove from the heat. When the sauce has cooled to lukewarm, discard the bouquet garni and add the egg yolks and butter, incorporating them gradually, until the mixture is smooth. Season with the salt and pepper. To finish the sauce, stir in the chopped herbs.

Tartar Sauce
Sauce tartare
This sauce can be served as an accompaniment to every type of fish, as well as cold cuts and cold chicken.

Makes 1 cup

3 hardboiled eggs
2 tablespoons Dijon mustard
1 tablespoon white vinegar
3 shallots, chopped
2 sprigs parsley or chervil, finely chopped
6 green onions or 2 sprigs tarragon, finely chopped
4 tablespoons vegetable oil
¼ teaspoon salt
¼ teaspoon pepper
1 tablespoon capers

Mash the hardboiled egg yolks with the mustard, vinegar, chopped herbs and shallots. Add the oil drop by drop, beating after each addition. Season with the salt and pepper and stir the capers into the sauce.

Hollandaise Sauce
Sauce hollandaise
Makes 1 cup

1 cup unsalted butter, cut into small pieces
2 egg yolks
½ teaspoon salt
1 tablespoon white wine vinegar or lemon juice
⅓ cup whipped cream (optional)

Melt the butter with the egg yolks, salt and vinegar over very low heat or in a double boiler, stirring constantly until the butter has melted. Continue stirring gently over low heat until the sauce thickens; do not let it boil. For a richer sauce, beat in whipped cream just before serving.

Horseradish Sauce

Sauce raifort, dite Radimsky

Makes 1 cup

5 hardboiled eggs
½ cup minced horseradish
3 small onions, finely chopped
2 tablespoons finely chopped chives
½ cup chopped parsley
1 tablespoon finely chopped chervil
¼ teaspoon salt
¼ teaspoon pepper
1 tablespoon capers
4 tablespoons Rich Broth (recipe on page 113)
1 tablespoon wine vinegar
2 teaspoons olive oil

Mash the egg yolks with the horseradish. Chop the egg whites finely and mix them into the horseradish mixture. Combine the chopped onions and chives with the chopped herbs, salt and pepper. Add this mixture to the egg-and-horseradish mixture and combine well. Add the capers. Stir in the Rich Broth and wine vinegar and bind with the olive oil.

Mayonnaise

Sauce mayonnaise

This mayonnaise is served with cold chicken or fish. To make a really good mayonnaise you need to stir the mixture rhythmically and have lots of patience.

Makes about 1 ¼ cups

1 egg yolk
¼ teaspoon salt
¼ teaspoon pepper
About 1 teaspoon lemon juice or white wine vinegar
1 cup olive oil
1 tablespoon finely chopped chervil (optional)
1 tablespoon finely chopped chives (optional)

Mayonnaise should be made two hours before it is needed, so that the flavors combine well. Put the egg yolk, salt, pepper, and lemon juice or vinegar into a bowl. Stir with a metal spoon. Add the oil, drop by drop, stirring well after each addition. Once the sauce has thickened, taste it and add more lemon juice or vinegar if necessary. Chervil or chives can be added at this stage.

Fresh Tomato Sauce

Sauce tomate

Makes 1 cup

6 large, ripe tomatoes, peeled
1 sprig thyme
1 bayleaf
¼ teaspoon salt
¼ teaspoon pepper
2 tablespoons unsalted butter
½ cup diced lean ham (optional)

Cut the tomatoes into quarters and press them lightly to remove excess juice. Discard the seeds. Put the tomatoes into a saucepan with the thyme and bayleaf; do not cover. Season with the salt and pepper. Bring to the boil and as soon as the tomatoes begin to boil, reduce the heat. Simmer them, uncovered, until they form a purée. Pass them through a sieve and keep the sauce warm in a bain-marie (water bath). Add the butter to the tomato sauce just before serving, as well as the diced lean ham, if desired.

Pages 120-121:
Onions and shallots were finely chopped
to make the white butter sauce to
accompany the Sunday pike (recipe on page 157).

Appetizers and Side Dishes

Welsh Rarebit

Welsh Rarebit (recette anglaise)

Serves 10

10 large slices day-old bread, about ½ inch thick
7 ounces Cheddar cheese, thinly sliced
4 tablespoons beer
1 heaping tablespoon French mustard
½ teaspoon pepper
½ cup unsalted butter

Trim the crusts from the slices of bread and make them into neat rectangles. Toast them evenly on both sides and keep them warm.

Meanwhile, in a skillet over low heat, cook the cheese with the beer and mustard, stirring constantly to prevent boiling. Season with the pepper. Quickly butter each slice of toast and pour a tablespoon of the cheese mixture over it. Serve very hot.

Charlotte Lysès's Stuffed White Onions

Oignons blancs farcis (Charlotte Lysès)

This dish is delicious served either hot or cold.

Serves 4

4 large white onions
1 cup ground cooked roast pork, chicken or calves' liver
2 tablespoons chopped chives
2 tablespoons dried mixed herbs
½ cup grated Gruyère cheese
1 hardboiled egg

Cut ½-inch slices off the tops of the onions. Blanch the onions, by putting them into boiling water to cover and cooking for 30 minutes. Drain and cool. Scoop out the center of each, leaving about a ½ inch wall. Combine the ground cooked meat with the chives, dried mixed herbs, and half the grated cheese. Mash the egg yolk and chop the white; combine them with the rest of

Opposite: One of the recipes Monet adopted, Charlotte Lysès's stuffed white onions (recipe on this page).

the mixture. Stuff the onions with the mixture, mounding it slightly above the level of the onions.

Preheat the oven to 350°. Place the onions in a greased roasting pan and sprinkle with the rest of the grated Gruyère cheese. Bake for 30 minutes or until the cheese is lightly browned.

Baked Kidney Beans

Haricots rouges à l'étuvée

Serves 6

2 ¼ cups kidney beans
1 teaspoon salt
1 or 2 medium-size onions, cut into quarters
2 sprigs thyme
1 bayleaf
1 ½ tablespoons lard
4 ounces bacon or pancetta, sliced
4 thick slices smoked ham
6 frankfurters
1 cup dry red wine

Cover the kidney beans with water and soak for 6 hours or overnight. Drain. Put the beans into a deep pot with a lid and add water to cover. Add the salt and onions, thyme and bayleaf. Bring the water to a boil. Half-cover the pot and boil for 10 minutes, then reduce the heat until the liquid just simmers. Cook gently for about 2 hours, covered. The beans should swell but must not burst. When they are soft to the touch but not completely cooked through, strain them, reserving the cooking liquid. Discard the thyme and bayleaf and cover the beans to prevent them from drying out.

In a large pot with a tight-fitting lid, heat the lard. Add the bacon, ham and frankfurters and sauté until golden but not browned. Add the beans, red wine and about 4 cups of the bean cooking liquid. Cover the pot with a piece of parchment paper larger than the diameter of the pot, then place the lid on top, to keep all the steam inside. Cook over low heat for about 2 hours, or until the liquid is very much reduced. You can check on the progress of the cooking from time to time, but do not stir the contents of the pot.

Stéphane Mallarmé's Recipe for Chanterelles

Recette de girolles (Mallarmé)

These wild mushrooms are just as good, maybe even better, when reheated in a bain-marie (water bath) or double boiler.

Serves 8

2 ½ pounds fresh chanterelle mushrooms
4 ounces bacon or pancetta
3 ½ tablespoons lard
½ teaspoon pepper
1 garlic clove, minced
2 tablespoons chopped parsley

Trim the stems of the mushrooms and wipe them to remove the sand, but avoid washing them, if possible. Cut the largest ones in half. Chop the bacon or pancetta into small pieces. Melt the lard in a skillet and add the chopped bacon. Sauté the bacon and sprinkle it with pepper.

Add the chanterelles and cook them over low heat for 1 ½ hours, or until the liquid from the chanterelles has evaporated. Add the garlic and parsley and cook for another 5 minutes.

Poached Truffles

Truffes à la serviette

Serves 4

4 truffles
4 thin slices bacon
About 2 cups dry white wine
Unsalted butter (to serve)

Wash the truffles thoroughly, rubbing them with a brush, and peel them slightly. Place the bacon in a deep pot and place the truffles on top. Add enough white wine to cover them. Cover the pot and cook over medium heat for 35 minutes.

Drain the truffles. Lay them inside a warmed serviette so that it covers them, and lay it on a warmed platter. Serve with melted unsalted butter.

My Recipe for Cèpes

Ma recette pour les cèpes

This dish is even more delicious when reheated.

Serves 4

1 pound cèpes (wild mushrooms)
4 tablespoons olive oil
2 garlic cloves, minced
4 sprigs parsley, chopped
½ teaspoon salt
½ teaspoon pepper

Wipe and peel the cèpes. Discard the tip of the stem and chop the stems finely with a knife, leaving the caps whole. Arrange the stems in a shallow ovenproof dish and lay the caps on top of them. Sprinkle with the olive oil.

Preheat the oven to 325°. Bake the cèpes for 20 minutes, or until the oil is transparent. Combine the garlic and parsley. Remove the cèpes from the oven and sprinkle the mixture over them. Season them with salt and pepper. Return the cèpes to the oven and bake for another 20 minutes, basting at least twice with the liquid in the dish.

Opposite: An extract from the journals on how to prepare chanterelle mushrooms (recipe on this page).

Recettes des Girolles

Coupez les queues des champignons et partagez les gros en deux. Laissez les tremper une heure dans de l'eau afin que le sable se détache, lavez les ensuite à plusieurs eaux et laissez égoutter.

Prenez, pour 1 kg. de girolles, un demi quart de lard de poitrine haché, un bon morceau de saindoux, dans lequel vous faites revenir le lard. Mettez y les champignons et un peu de poivre et peu de sel (le lard sale presque suffisamment)

Laissez cuire environ 1 heure et demie afin que l'eau que jettent les girolles soit réduite complètement. Cinq minutes avant de servir prenez une gousse d'ail. hachée menue avec du persil que vous mettez dans les champignons

Les girolles sont aussi bonnes, presque meilleures qu'à la première fois, réchauffées au bain-marie

Stuffed Tomatoes

Tomates farcies

Serves 4

4 large, ripe tomatoes
1 sprig parsley
1 sprig thyme
1 bayleaf
1 sprig chervil
¼ teaspoon salt
¼ teaspoon pepper
1 cup fresh breadcrumbs
2 tablespoons vegetable oil
1 cup chopped bacon
2 tablespoons chopped parsley
1 garlic clove, minced
2 shallots, minced
2 egg yolks
4 mushrooms, finely chopped (optional)

Cut ½-inch slices off the bottoms of the tomatoes. Scoop out the center of each, leaving a ½ inch wall. Place the pulp in a saucepan and cook it over high heat. When it has boiled for about 3 minutes, remove the pan from the heat and press the contents through a sieve. Pour the purée thus obtained into the saucepan.

Tie the parsley, thyme, bayleaf, and chervil together in a piece of cheesecloth to make a bouquet garni. Add it to the pan. Season with the salt and pepper. Cook for about 15 minutes over low heat, uncovered, to thicken the purée. Discard the bouquet garni and stir in the breadcrumbs. Cook for 3 minutes.

Heat the oil in a skillet. Combine the bacon, parsley, garlic and shallots, and sauté the mixture in the oil, stirring occasionally, until the bacon is lightly browned. Add half the tomato and breadcrumb mixture. Mix well and stir in the egg yolks to bind the mixture. At this stage, the mushrooms can be added if desired.

Preheat the oven to 350°. Stuff the tomatoes with the bacon-and-herb mixture. Place them in a greased ovenproof dish and pour the rest of the tomato and breadcrumb mixture over them. Bake for 30 minutes or until the tops are lightly browned.

Baked Field Mushrooms

Gratin de champignons

Serves 4

4 cups (about ½ pound) fresh field or cultivated mushrooms
¼ cup unsalted butter
1 tablespoon chopped shallots
1 tablespoon cognac
1 scant tablespoon flour
2 tablespoons heavy cream or crème fraîche
½ teaspoon salt
½ teaspoon pepper

Trim off the muddy tips of the mushroom stems and carefully wipe the mushrooms to remove sand, but avoid washing them if possible. Slice them into quarters, slicing the largest mushrooms once more.

Melt the butter in a saucepan. Add the shallots. Cover the saucepan and cook for 10 minutes over medium heat. Add the cognac and cook for 2 minutes. Preheat the oven to 450°. Meanwhile, combine the flour and cream, pour this mixture over the mushrooms and continue to cook, stirring continually, for about 5 minutes more. Season with the salt and pepper and pour into a gratin dish or ovenproof dish. Bake for about 15 minutes or until lightly browned.

Potato Pie

Pâté de pommes de terre

Serves 8

½ pound savory pie dough
6 medium-size potatoes, peeled and cut into thin rounds
4 medium-size onions, thinly sliced
½ cup chopped parsley
½ teaspoon salt
½ teaspoon pepper
3 tablespoons heavy cream or crème fraîche
1 egg, beaten

Grease an 8-inch pie pan. Roll out half the dough and use it to cover the base and sides of the pan. Arrange the potato rounds in the pan, and cover with the onion rings and the parsley. Sprinkle with the salt and pepper and add the cream.

Roll out the rest of the dough and use it to make a lid for the pie. Arrange the pastry lid over the pie and make a hole in the center. Roll a small piece of cardboard into a tube to make a funnel-shaped pie chimney; this is essential to allow the steam to escape during cooking.

Preheat the oven to 350°. Brush the dough with the beaten egg and bake the pie for 1 ½−2 hours. If it browns too soon, cover with greased parchment paper.

Glazed Carrots

Carottes fermières

This dish is very good served with braised meat.

Serves 4

3 cups sliced raw carrots
1 tablespoon unsalted butter
1 tablespoon flour
2 sprigs chervil,chopped
4 sprigs parsley, chopped
1 sprig tarragon, chopped
½ teaspoon salt
½ teaspoon pepper
1 cup Rich Broth (recipe on page 113)
Juice of ½ lemon
1 tablespoon confectioner's sugar

Cook the carrots in 3 cups boiling water for 10 minutes, or until almost cooked. Drain them, reserving the cooking liquid.

In a saucepan with a lid, melt the butter and stir the flour into it. Cook for 2 minutes, stirring, then add the chopped herbs, salt and pepper, ¼ cup of the carrot cooking liquid, and the Rich Broth. Add the lemon juice and confectioner's sugar, and finally the carrots. Bring to a boil, then reduce the heat to very low and place the pan half-off the heat, so that the contents cook very slowly. Half-cover the pan to allow the steam to escape during cooking. Cook for 1 hour, or until the carrots are cooked and glazed. Serve in a warmed vegetable dish.

Stuffed Eggplant

Aubergines farcies

This dish is served accompanied by Fresh Tomato Sauce (recipe on page 119).

Serves 4

4 large eggplants
1 tablespoon coarse salt
About 6 tablespoons flour
1 cup olive oil
2 cups chopped mushrooms
½ cup chopped parsley
1 or 2 shallots, chopped
1 or 2 garlic cloves, chopped
½ teaspoon salt
½ teaspoon pepper
1 tablespoon tomato paste
¼ cup unsalted butter
2 cups dry breadcrumbs

Split the eggplants lengthwise. Make a few cuts in the flesh and sprinkle them with the coarse salt. Leave them for about one hour.

Rinse the eggplants, pat them dry, and coat them with the flour, dusting off the excess. Heat the oil in a skillet and sauté the eggplants until they are cooked through, but still firm. Drain them, reserving the oil. When they are cool, scoop out the flesh, taking care not to damage the skins. Coarsely chop the flesh.

Combine the mushrooms, parsley, shallots, and garlic cloves and season them with the salt and pepper. Heat the oil again and add the mixture to the skillet, cooking until the mushrooms are softened. Stir in the tomato paste and the eggplant flesh. Stuff this mixture back into the eggplant skins. Arrange them in a shallow, buttered baking dish.

In a small skillet, melt the butter and add the breadcrumbs, stirring until they are golden. Preheat the broiler.

Sprinkle the breadcrumb mixture over the eggplants, and broil them under high heat until the breadcrumbs are just beginning to brown.

Serve with Fresh Tomato Sauce.

Baked Beans Provençal-Style

Haricots secs à la provençale

Lentils and other dried legumes may be cooked in much the same way as the Baked Kidney Beans (page 123). They should be soaked overnight, like the beans, in water to cover, which is discarded before cooking.

Serves 8

8 cups presoaked navy or great northern beans
1 cup Rich Broth (recipe on page 113)
4 tablespoons olive oil
2 tablespoons unsalted butter
2 onions, thinly sliced
4 sprigs parsley, chopped
1 bouquet garni
1 preserved goose thigh
½ teaspoon salt
½ teaspoon pepper
¼ teaspoon nutmeg

Preheat the oven to 350°. Put the beans, Rich Broth, oil, butter, onions, parsley, bouquet garni and goose thigh into an ovenproof pot with a tight-fitting lid. Season with the salt, pepper, and nutmeg. Bake for at least 4 hours, so that the beans will be cooked and the sauce reduced and thickened.

Cèpes Bordeaux-Style

Cèpes à la bordelaise

Serves 8

2 ½ pounds fresh cèpes (wild mushrooms)
About 2 cups vegetable oil
½ teaspoon pepper
½ teaspoon salt
2 cups fine, dry breadcrumbs
2 garlic cloves, minced
4 sprigs parsley, chopped

Clean the cèpes well, but do not wash them. Separate the caps from the stems. Heat the oil in a pan; there must be enough to cover the cèpes. As soon as the oil is hot, add the cèpes. Sprinkle them with the pepper. Cook them for at least 1 hour, uncovered, over low heat. Drain them, reserving 2 tablespoons of oil in the pan. Sprinkle the cèpes with salt. Arrange on a heated serving platter.

While the cèpes are cooking, press the dry breadcrumbs through a sieve and mix them with the garlic and parsley. Heat the reserved oil in the pan and add the breadcrumb mixture. Cook briefly, stirring, over high heat, but do not let it brown. Arrange the breadcrumb mixture in a circle around the cèpes. Serve very hot.

Stuffed Artichoke Hearts

Fonds d'artichauts farcis

Serves 6

6 artichokes
6 slices bacon
2 medium-size onions
4 to 6 shallots
1 garlic clove
4 cups mushrooms
1 tablespoon Tomato Sauce (recipe on page 118)
¼ teaspoon salt
2 tablespoons vegetable oil
½ cup unsalted butter
1 ½ cups broth
2 cups dry breadcrumbs

Trim the leaves away from the artichokes. Wrap each choke in a slice of bacon, tied securely. Place in a deep pot of boiling water to cover. Cook for about 20 minutes, or until the hearts are soft. Discard the bacon.

Chop the onions, shallots, garlic, and mushrooms. Add the Tomato Sauce and salt. Pour the oil into a skillet and add half the butter. When hot, add the chopped mixture and sauté for 5 minutes. Add the broth and cook, uncovered over high heat, until the mixture thickens, about 10 minutes. Use the mixture to stuff the artichokes. Arrange them on a greased baking dish.

In a small skillet, melt the rest of the butter and add the breadcrumbs, stirring until they are golden. Preheat the broiler. Sprinkle the breadcrumb mixture over the artichokes. Broil them under high heat until the breadcrumbs are just beginning to brown.

Eggplant and Tomato

Aubergines aux tomates

Serves 8

12 eggplants
Coarse salt
12 medium-size, ripe tomatoes
½ cup unsalted butter
1 sprig thyme
1 clove
6 shallots, minced
3 sprigs parsley, chopped
2 chervil leaves, chopped
1 sprig tarragon, chopped
1 or 2 garlic cloves, minced
2 tablespoons vegetable oil
½ cup dry breadcrumbs

Slice the eggplants, but do not peel them. Sprinkle them with coarse salt and leave them for 1 hour. Peel the tomatoes, discarding the centers and seeds. Melt half the butter in a saucepan, add the tomatoes and cook until they are soft. Tie the thyme and clove in a piece of cheesecloth. Put the tomatoes into a saucepan and add the thyme and clove tied in the cheesecloth, shallots, parsley, chervil, tarragon, and garlic. Cook, covered, for 15 minutes. Discard the thyme and clove in the cheesecloth.

Preheat the oven to 325°. Pour the oil into a deep ovenproof dish. Arrange a layer of eggplant over it, then a layer of tomato, then another layer of eggplant, and so on, until all the tomato and eggplant have been used up. Sprinkle with the dry breadcrumbs and dot with the rest of the butter. Bake for approximately 2 hours, or until the topping is golden.

Mushroom Purée

Purée de champignons

Serves 4

¼ cup unsalted butter
Juice of ½ lemon
¼ teaspoon salt
2 cups thinly-sliced mushrooms
1 tablespoon flour
½ cup milk

Melt half the butter in a saucepan. Add 2 tablespoons hot water, the lemon juice and salt. As soon as the liquid boils, add the mushrooms. Cook them, covered, for about 10 minutes or until the juices run. Drain them, retaining the cooking liquid. Grind the mushrooms into a purée.

Melt the rest of the butter in the saucepan and, when it is hot, add the flour and stir well without letting it color. Add the milk and continue to stir well. When the liquid thickens, add about ½ cup of the mushroom cooking liquid. Cook, stirring occasionally, until the liquid is reduced by one third. Stir the mushroom purée into it and serve hot.

Poultry

Stuffed Capon

Chapon farci

Serves 10

4 tablespoons dry breadcrumbs (optional)
2 roasted onions
1 slice (4 ounces) cooked ham
1 chicken liver
1 chicken gizzard
1 cup sliced mushrooms
3 morels
½ teaspoon salt
½ teaspoon pepper
4 tablespoons heavy cream or crème fraîche
¼ cup unsalted butter
2 egg yolks
½ cup madeira wine
1 capon (at least 6½ pounds), with giblets
1 chicken neck
3 carrots
2 sprigs thyme
2 sprigs parsley

Soak the breadcrumbs, if you are using them, in milk, then squeeze to remove excess liquid. Chop the onions, ham, liver, chicken gizzard, mushrooms and morels. Mix well and add the salt and pepper. Bind with the cream. Melt half the butter in a saucepan and add the stuffing mixture. Cook, stirring constantly over low heat, until the mushrooms are soft, about 10 minutes. Remove from the heat and leave to cool before beating in the egg yolks and madeira. If the mixture is too liquid add the dry breadcrumbs.

Preheat the oven to 350°. Stuff the capon with the mixture, truss it tightly and place it in a roasting pan. Melt the rest of the butter and brush the skin with it. Pour enough water into the pan to come 1 inch up the sides. Arrange the chicken neck, carrots, and the thyme and parsley, tied together, around the capon. Roast for approximately 2 hours.

Opposite: The poultry was carefully selected, especially the Christmas capon (recipe for stuffed capon on this page).

Chicken in White Wine Sauce

Poulet à la périgourdine

Serves 4

4 tablespoons unsalted butter
1 roasting chicken (about 3 pounds), cut into serving pieces
6 shallots, 3 of them chopped
½ teaspoon salt
½ teaspoon pepper
½ cup dry white wine

Melt the butter in a large, deep skillet and sauté the chicken pieces. When they are nicely browned, remove and reserve them. Add the three chopped and three whole shallots to the pan. When they have begun to brown, return the chicken and any cooking juices to the pan. Sprinkle with the salt and pepper. Reduce the heat and cook for about 45 minutes, turning the pieces from time to time, until they are uniformly cooked through. As soon as the liquid begins to dry up, add the wine. Discard the whole shallots before serving hot.

Broiled Chicken

Poulet grillé

Serves 2-4

1 small (2-3 pounds) grain-fed chicken
½ teaspoon salt
½ teaspoon pepper
½ cup melted unsalted butter
4 tablespoons chopped parsley, or 1 cup watercress
4 slices lemon

Preheat the oven to 400°. Split the chicken lengthwise along the backbone, and flatten the two chicken halves. Salt and pepper them on the cavity side. Place them in a roasting pan, skin side up and coat with half the melted butter. Roast for 15 minutes.

Preheat the broiler to maximum, then place the pan under the broiler. Broil, for about 45 minutes, turning from time to time so that it is evenly browned all over. Pour the rest of the melted butter over the chicken, and garnish with parsley or watercress, and lemon slices.

Baked Chicken

Poulet en cocotte

Serves 6

4 tablespoons unsalted butter
4 slices lean bacon, chopped into pieces
2 onions, thinly sliced
1 roasting chicken (about 3 pounds), trussed
1 cup dry white wine
½ teaspoon salt
½ teaspoon pepper
1 cup sliced mushrooms

Preheat the oven to 325°. Melt the butter in a deep, flameproof casserole with a tight-fitting lid. Add the pieces of lean bacon and the onions. Sauté until they are nicely browned. Remove them from the pan and replace them with the chicken. Brown the chicken all over. Return the bacon and onions to the pan and add the white wine. Season with salt and pepper. Cover the pot and seal it hermetically with a piece of cheesecloth dipped in a flour-and-water paste.

Bake the chicken in the oven for 2 hours. Remove the pot from the oven, untruss the chicken and add the mushrooms. Replace the lid tightly, but do not seal and return the pot to the oven for another 20 minutes.

Fried Chicken

Poulet frit

This is a good way of using up leftover roast chicken.

Serves 4

2 cups flour
1 egg
1/8 teaspoon salt
4 pieces cooked chicken
2 cups vegetable oil

Combine the flour, egg, 1 cup water and salt to make a thick batter. It is essential to let it rest for at least 2 hours before use.

Dip the cooked chicken in the batter, coating it evenly. Heat the oil in a deep skillet. Test the heat by putting a small piece of chicken in it. If it bubbles and browns quickly, the oil is hot enough. Add the rest of the chicken pieces, turning frequently to make sure that they brown evenly.

Chicken Chasseur

Poulet chasseur

The fresh tomatoes can be replaced with double the quantity of tomato paste.

Serves 4

4 tablespoons unsalted butter
About 4 tablespoons vegetable oil
1 medium-size grain-fed chicken, cut into serving pieces
4 cups mushrooms, thinly sliced lengthwise
1 cup dry white wine
3 tomatoes, peeled, seeded and sliced
About 1 tablespoon tomato paste
½ teaspoon salt
½ teaspoon pepper
1 sprig tarragon
1 cup broth

Melt the butter with 4 tablespoons of the oil in a deep skillet with a lid. Sauté the chicken pieces until they are lightly colored. Reserve them. If there is not enough fat left in the pot, add another tablespoon of oil. Add the mushrooms. When their juices begin to run, add the wine.

Put the tomato slices into a saucepan and cook for 10 minutes, or until they are soft and the liquid is reduced. Add them to the mushrooms with the tomato paste. Season with the salt and pepper and add the tarragon. Cook, uncovered, for 10 minutes, to reduce the liquid. Add the broth and simmer, uncovered, for another 10 minutes.

Return the chicken and its cooking liquid to the skillet. Cover and cook over medium heat for 1 hour. Arrange the chicken on a serving platter and keep it warm. If the sauce appears to be too thin, reduce it by boiling it uncovered for 10 minutes. Pour it over the chicken before serving.

Braised Chicken in Red Wine

Coq au vin

This dish is excellent if left to cool, refrigerated and then reheated in a bain-marie.

Serves 4

½ cup unsalted butter
1 cup diced lean bacon
12 pearl onions
1 boiling fowl (about 5 pounds), cut into serving pieces
1 garlic clove
1 bouquet garni
6 cups mushrooms
4 tablespoons brandy
2 cups burgundy
2 tablespoons flour
Fried ½-inch croutons

Melt half the butter in a Dutch oven or flameproof casserole with a lid and sauté the bacon pieces and pearl onions until the onions are transparent. Remove and reserve the bacon and onions. Sauté the chicken pieces, turning them several times as they cook. Add the garlic clove, bouquet garni, and the mushrooms (if any are rather large, slice them in half). Cover the casserole and cook for 15 minutes. Skim off the surface fat.

Add the brandy and flame. Add the burgundy. Cover the casserole and cook for another 35 minutes. To check whether the chicken pieces are cooked, prick them with a fork. If the juice runs clear, they are cooked; if the juices are pink, continue cooking. When the chicken is cooked, drain it over the casserole and keep it warm.

Combine the rest of the butter with the flour until you have a smooth paste. Break off bits of it, and stir them into the sauce, stirring until each has melted before adding the next. As soon as the sauce is thick and smooth, return the pieces of chicken to it. Garnish the chicken with the fried croutons.

Chicken in Aspic

Poulet en gelée

Serves 6

1 pound leg of veal
1 pound knuckle of veal
2 pork rinds (about 4 ounces each)
1 bouquet garni
2 carrots, sliced (optional)
2 onions, thinly sliced (optional)
2 egg whites
½ cup Madeira wine
1 roasting chicken (about 3 pounds)
4 tablespoons unsalted butter

On the day before, make a consommé by cooking the meat and pork rinds with the bouquet garni, and carrots and onions, if desired, in water to cover. Bring to a boil and simmer, covered, for 6 hours, adding more water if necessary during the cooking. Strain and reserve this liquid. Leave it to cool, then degrease it. (This requires a certain amount of time, and it is recommended that you put the bowl of liquid in the coldest place possible.)

Reheat the liquid. Beat the egg whites into stiff peaks and add them to the liquid with the Madeira to clarify it. If the broth does not become very clear, repeat the operation, then leave the broth to cool.

Preheat the oven to 350°. Dot the chicken with the butter, then roast it, basting it every 15 minutes, first with ½ cup of the broth, and then with its own cooking liquid, for 2 hours. Do not let it brown too much or dry out. When the chicken is cooked, remove it from the oven and cool to room temperature. Remove and discard the skin and cut the chicken into serving pieces.

Pour some of the broth into a terrine, then add some chicken pieces. Add some more broth and more pieces, until all the chicken pieces are in the terrine. Cover the terrine with a double layer of cheesecloth and refrigerate it. To serve, arrange the pieces of chicken on a platter.

Chicken with Chervil

Poulet au cerfeuil

Serves 4-6

4 tablespoons vegetable oil or lard
1 roasting chicken (3–4 pounds), cut into serving pieces
1 parsley sprig
1 clove
1 bayleaf
1 sprig thyme
1 ¼ cups dry white wine
½ teaspoon salt
½ teaspoon pepper
4 tablespoons unsalted butter, softened
4 tablespoons flour
½ cup minced fresh chervil

Heat the oil or lard in a large deep skillet. When it begins to smoke, add the pieces of chicken and brown evenly all over. Tie the parsley, clove, bayleaf, and thyme in a piece of cheesecloth to make a bouquet garni, and add it to the pan. Add the wine, season and cook over medium heat until some of the liquid has evaporated and the chicken is cooked through. Discard the bouquet garni. Remove the chicken pieces and keep them hot.

Beat the butter and flour together with the chervil. Stir the chicken sauce, and while stirring, break off pieces of the chervil butter and incorporate it into the sauce. When the chervil butter has all been incorporated, remove the sauce from the heat and pour it over the chicken. Serve very hot.

Chicken with Crayfish Butter

Poulet au beurre d'écrevisses

Serves 6

1 cup unsalted butter, softened
4 cups (1 pound) crayfish shells , tails and legs
2 cups dry white wine
2 carrots, sliced in half
2 small onions
1 bouquet garni
½ teaspoon salt
½ teaspoon pepper
1 roasting chicken (about 3 pounds), trussed
1 tablespoon cornstarch

To make the crayfish butter, beat the butter with 2 tablespoons hot water until you have a smooth cream. Grind the crayfish shells, tails and legs, then pass them through a sieve. Mix the purée thus obtained with the butter.

Make broth in a deep pot, by heating the wine with 2 cups cold water, and adding the carrots, onions, bouquet garni, salt, and pepper. When the liquid boils, add the chicken and reduce the heat. Cook over medium heat for 1 hour.

Put the crayfish butter into a saucepan. Remove 1 cup of the cooking liquid from the pot and stir the cornstarch into it. Add this to the crayfish butter and stir until the liquid is smooth and thickened, but be careful not to let it boil.

Remove the chicken from the broth and pour the crayfish sauce over it before serving. Serve very hot.

Opposite: The recipe for chicken with crayfish butter from the cooking journals (recipe on this page).

ferme. Faites chauffer votre fer à gauffres,
roulez un morceau de pâte de la grosseur
que vous voudrez (selon la grandeur du
gaufrier sujet à brûler)

Poulet au beurre d'écrivisses.

Prenez un beau poulet blanc, faites le
cuire avec du bouillon ou de jus, un peu
de champignons, un peu de citron pour
empêcher le poulet de noircir; prenez une
douzaine d'écrevisses, faites les cuire à l'étouffée
avec un peu de beurre, carottes et échalote;
pilez-les avec un bon morceau de beurre, faites
les revenir au beurre dans une casserole,
mouillez avec du jus du poulet, passez au
tamis; faites fondre du beurre, mettez un
peu de farine ajoutez le jus des écrevisses,
faites les cuire toujours en remuant
la sauce et quand elle est cuite
au tour du poulet

Meat

Cold Beef à la Mode
(Marthe Butler's Recipe)

Boeuf mode (Marthe Butler)

Marthe Butler's recipe is an adaptation of a classic French dish, which involves larding a boneless round beef roast with strips of bacon, marinating it in white wine and brandy, then braising it for several hours with a pig's or calf's foot to make the cooking liquid jell. The meat is served cold, garnished with baby vegetables and aspic made from the strained and clarified meat cooking liquid.

Serves 8

¼ cup unsalted butter
4-5 slices bacon
2 ½ pounds boneless round beef roast
3 cups meat juices or broth
3 cups dry white wine
5 carrots
1 onion, chopped
2 tablespoons brandy

Melt the butter in a deep pot and sauté the bacon in it. When the fat begins to melt, add the roast and brown it on both sides. Remove and reserve it. Add 1 cup of the meat juices or broth, and 1 cup of the wine, the carrots and onion. Return the meat to the liquid, cover and cook over very low heat. While it is cooking, gradually add the rest of the meat juices or broth and the wine. Cook for 6 hours, then add the brandy. The meat should cook for at least 7 hours.

Let it cool to room temperature before removing it from the pot.

Opposite: Marthe Butler's version of the classic dish, cold beef à la mode, was served on Sunday on the blue Creil china (recipe on this page).

Pages 138-139: The preparation of cold beef à la mode required some planning. The meat had to cook for seven hours. Fresh vegetables were ordered from Florimond the day before they were required.

Beef Pie

Pâté de boeuf

Serves 6

4 ounces lean ground chuck
1 onion
1 garlic clove
5 tomatoes, peeled, seeded, and roughly chopped
½ cup parsley
½ cup fresh tarragon
2 ounces bacon
¼ teaspoon grated nutmeg
1 teaspoon salt
1 teaspoon pepper
4 tablespoons unsalted butter
2 cups flour
¼ cup lard
1 egg yolk, beaten

Grind the beef again with the onion, garlic, tomatoes, parsley, tarragon, and bacon. Add the grated nutmeg. Season with half the salt, and all the pepper. Melt half the butter in a skillet and sauté the mixture, stirring frequently, making sure that the mixture remains moist. Pour it into a dish and leave to cool to room temperature.

Make the pastry dough by combining the flour with the lard, about 1 cup water and the rest of the salt. Roll it into a ball, wrap it in a damp cloth and let it rest in a cool place for 20 minutes. Roll it out with a rolling pin, then roll it in a ball again, wrap it in a damp cloth and let it rest for 20 minutes. Repeat the process once more. Then roll out half the dough to fit the bottom and sides of an 8-inch greased pie pan. Fill the pan with the beef mixture, then roll out the rest of the dough to form a lid for the pie.

Preheat the oven to 375°. Brush the dough with the beaten egg yolk. Make a hole in the center of the pie and roll up a small piece of cardboard to make a funnel through which the steam can escape. Insert the funnel in the hole. Bake the pie for approximately 1 hour or until it is golden-brown.

Stuffed Shoulder of Lamb

Epaule de mouton farcie

Serves 6

1 boned shoulder of lamb (about 3 pounds)
1 teaspoon salt
1 teaspoon pepper
4 tablespoons fat
8 medium-size onions, thinly sliced
2 cups partially cooked navy beans
4 potatoes, peeled and thickly sliced

Stuffing

4 tablespoons fresh breadcrumbs soaked in milk
1 slice lean bacon, chopped
2 tablespoons chopped parsley
2 garlic cloves, minced
½ teaspoon salt
½ teaspoon pepper

Squeeze the breadcrumbs dry. Combine the stuffing ingredients. Lay the shoulder out flat. Season with half the salt and pepper, then spread the stuffing over it. Roll it up, using a strip of cheesecloth and tie firmly. Melt the fat in a large pot with a lid, and brown the meat evenly. Surround it with the onions, beans, and potatoes. Season with the rest of the salt and pepper. Add hot water to cover.

Preheat the oven to 350°. Cover the pot with the lid and bring to a boil on top of the stove. Transfer to the oven and continue cooking for at least 2 hours.

Broiled Steak with Mustard

Entrecôte à la briarde

Serves 1

1 filet steak (about 8 ounces)
4 tablespoons Meaux mustard
2 tablespoons unsalted butter

Spread both sides of the steak with the mustard, and leave for 2 hours. Melt the butter in a skillet or steak pan and sauté the steak on both sides.

Sacha Guitry's Shoulder of Pork

Palette de porc Sacha (Guitry)

Serves 8 to 10

1 shoulder of pork (about 5 pounds)
1 tablespoon coarse salt
1 teaspoon black pepper
1 bouquet garni
1 cabbage, trimmed, leaves separated
8 potatoes, peeled and cut into quarters
1 garlic-flavored boiling sausage (about 1 pound)

Put the pork into a deep pot and add water to cover. Add the salt, pepper, and bouquet garni. Bring the water to a boil and when it boils add the cabbage and potatoes. Cover the pot and simmer for 2 hours. Add the sausage, and cook for another 30 minutes. Serve.

Lucien Guitry's Lamb Stew

Cassoulet de Guitry (Lucien)

Serves 8

2 cups dried white beans (Great Northern or navy)
2 pounds boneless shoulder or leg of lamb, bite-size pieces
1 pound smoked breast of goose
4 ounces chopped pork fat, fatback or blanched salt pork
1 tablespoon flour
4 cups chicken or beef broth
1 teaspoon salt
½ teaspoon pepper
1 bouquet garni
1 garlic clove, chopped
2 tablespoons tomato paste
1 large (1 pound) garlic-flavored boiling sausage
4 tablespoons chopped parsley
½ cup dry breadcrumbs

Soak the beans overnight in water to cover, then drain. Put the meat and pork fat into a large skillet and sauté until well browned, turning frequently. Transfer the meat to a tinned copper pot or flameproof covered casserole.

Sprinkle the meats with the flour, stir and pour in the broth. Season with the salt and pepper and add the bouquet garni, garlic, and tomato paste. Boil 3 cups water in a saucepan. Add the sausage and poach it on very low heat for 20 minutes, or until cooked through. Cut it into 2-inch pieces and add it to the stew.

Parboil the beans in water to cover for 10 minutes. Drain them and add them to the stew. Cover it and simmer it for at least 2 hours.

Preheat the oven to 400°. Remove the lid from the pot, sprinkle with the parsley and breadcrumbs and place in the oven. Cook for 30 minutes or until well browned on top. Serve in the casserole, if possible.

Beef Tongue au Gratin

Langue de boeuf au gratin

Serves 8

1 beef tongue
2 carrots
3 onions
4 black peppercorns
1 bouquet garni
1 cup dry white wine
3 pickled cucumbers, sliced
3 chopped shallots
4 tablespoons chopped parsley
1 cup dry breadcrumbs
4 tablespoons unsalted butter, cut into pieces

The day before, soak the tongue in cold water to cover. The next day, blanch it in boiling water to cover for 30 minutes. Remove it and drain it. Take out the bones and trim away the fat, then peel the tongue. Place in cold water with the carrots, onions, peppercorns, and the bouquet garni. Bring to a boil, cover, then cook at a bare simmer for 3 hours.

Remove the tongue from the liquid. Once it is cool, slice it thinly at a slight angle. Preheat the oven to 325°. Grease a large, ovenproof dish. Arrange the slices of tongue on it and sprinkle them with the wine. Arrange the slices of pickled cucumber over them. Sprinkle with the dry breadcrumbs and dot it with the butter. Bake for 30 minutes or until lightly browned.

Pork Chops Foyot

Escalopes Foyot

Serves 4

8 tablespoons unsalted butter
4 onions, thinly sliced
4 pork chops
½ cup dry breadcrumbs
½ cup grated Gruyère or Parmesan cheese
½ cup dry white wine
½ teaspoon salt
½ teaspoon pepper
4 lemon wedges

Melt half the butter in a skillet and sauté the onions until softened but not browned. Preheat the oven to 325°. Place the pork chops in a shallow, greased ovenproof dish. Pile the onions on top, then sprinkle with the breadcrumbs and grated cheese. Pour the white wine into the bottom of the dish. Cut the rest of the butter into pieces and dot over the mixture. Season. Bake the pork chops for 45 minutes or until the tops are golden. Serve garnished with lemon wedges.

Veal with Olives

Veau aux olives

Serves 4

4 tablespoons oil
1 small boned, rolled veal roast (about 2 ½ pounds)
2 cups green olives, pitted
36 pearl onions, peeled and trimmed
¼ teaspoon salt
½ teaspoon pepper
1 cup hot broth or water

Heat the oil in a casserole with a lid. Add the veal and brown all over. Cover and cook over low heat for 30 minutes. Add the olives and onions. Season with the salt and pepper. Add the broth or water to the cooking liquid. Serve the cooking liquid as a sauce with the veal, and garnish with the olives and onions.

Broiled Steak with Wine Sauce

Entrecôte marchand de vin

The same recipe can be used with white wine instead of red wine.

Serves 1

2 tablespoons unsalted butter
2 tablespoons flour
2 tablespoons broth
4 tablespoons dry red wine
2 chopped shallots
½ teaspoon salt
½ teaspoon pepper
1 filet steak (about 8 ounces)

Melt the butter in a saucepan and stir in the flour. When the mixture is smooth, add the broth. Remove from the heat. Pour the wine into another saucepan and add the shallots. Cook over high heat until the liquid is reduced by half. Strain the liquid and add it to the flour and butter mixture. Keep this sauce warm while you broil the steak on both sides. When the steak is cooked, coat it with the sauce.

Oxtail Stew (Marguéry's recipe)

Queue de boeuf en hochepot (Marguéry)

Serves 6

4 pork rinds (about 8 ounces)
2 sprigs thyme
1 bayleaf
3 pounds oxtail, cut into 6 portions
3 cups beef broth
1 cup dry white wine
4 tablespoons unsalted butter
12 pearl onions
1 tablespoon confectioner's sugar
5 cups button mushrooms
2 ½ pounds chestnuts
6 small frankfurter sausages

Arrange the pork rinds, thyme and bayleaf in a deep pot. Lay the oxtail on top. Cook over medium heat, uncovered, for 15 minutes. Moisten with 1 cup beef broth and cook until the liquid forms a glaze. Add the rest of the broth and the white wine. Cover the pot and cook over low heat for about 3 hours.

Meanwhile, melt half the butter and sauté the onions, adding the confectioner's sugar when they are transparent, stirring until they are glazed. In another saucepan, melt the rest of the butter and cook the mushrooms until the juices run. Cut crosses in the chestnut skins, then boil them in water to cover for 40 minutes. Peel, removing the inner and outer skins. Transfer the oxtail to a deep skillet. Strain the cooking liquid and degrease it. Add the onions, mushrooms, sausages, and chestnuts. Cook for 15 minutes and serve hot.

Pickled Beef

Boeuf berrichon

Serves 8

1 round boneless beef roast (about 5 pounds)
4 slices slab bacon, cut into strips
2 tablespoons wine vinegar
1 tablespoon white wine
1 garlic clove
2 shallots, each stuck with 1 clove
1 teaspoon salt
1 teaspoon pepper
4 tablespoons unsalted butter
About 3 cups broth or water
3 carrots (optional)

Lard the beef with the strips of bacon. Place it in a deep earthenware pot with the vinegar, white wine, garlic, and shallots. Season with the salt and pepper and cover it lightly with a piece of cheesecloth. Marinate for two days in the refrigerator, turning the meat twice a day.

Strain the marinade and reserve it. Melt the butter in a deep pot and sauté the beef on both sides. When it is nicely browned, moisten it with about 1 cup of the broth or water and 1 tablespoon of the marinade. Cover the pot and simmer over low heat for 6 hours, adding more broth or water and more marinade from time to time. The carrots should be added 1 hour before the end of the cooking time, if desired.

Yorkshire Pudding

Yorkshire pudding

In France, this traditional English accompaniment to roast beef is also eaten with roast lamb.

Serves 8

1 cup flour
3 eggs, beaten
2 cups cold milk
½ teaspoon salt
¼ teaspoon nutmeg

Preheat the oven to 450°. Grease a metal baking pan, ideally with fat from the roast meat. Put in the oven to get hot.

Sift the flour into a bowl, and make a well in the center.

Pour the beaten eggs into the well, then gradually incorporate the flour. Beat in the milk and season with the salt and nutmeg.

Pour the mixture into the heated baking pan.

Bake for about 25 minutes or until the Yorkshire pudding is well-risen and golden.

Sprinkle some meat juices over the pudding and serve it hot.

Baked Calves' Liver

Foie de veau à la moissoneuse

Serves 6

4 ounces bacon, coarsely chopped
½ cup olive oil
4 large onions, thinly sliced
10 medium-size potatoes
1 ½ pounds calves' liver
½ teaspoon salt
½ teaspoon pepper
1 cup dry red wine
½ cup broth
2 tablespoons unsalted butter
2 tablespoons flour
2 tablespoons chopped parsley
1 garlic clove, crushed

In a large skillet, sauté the bacon in the oil. When the fat begins to melt, remove it with a skimmer and arrange it on a serving platter. Continue to heat the oil, and when it is slightly smoking, add the onions and potatoes. Sauté them on low heat, while you cut the liver into 1-inch squares. Season them with the salt and pepper.

Remove the onions and potatoes from the skillet and arrange them on the platter with the bacon. Add the pieces of liver to the skillet, increase the heat and sauté quickly, turning frequently. Drain the liver and keep it warm, covered with a dish towel (a lid would hold the steam inside).

Discard the fat in the skillet and pour the wine into it. Deglaze the pan by scraping it to dislodge any bits that have stuck to the bottom and reduce the liquid by two-thirds over high heat. Add the broth and bring back to a boil. Combine the butter and flour into a smooth paste and break into pieces. Drop it into the sauce, stirring well after each addition. The sauce should be light. Add the onions, bacon, and potatoes and the chopped parsley and garlic. Cover the skillet and simmer for about 20 minutes.

Return the liver to the skillet, and cook, stirring, for 5 minutes, to reheat. Serve very hot.

Broiled Steak with Bone-Marrow Sauce

Entrecôte bordelaise

Serves 1

2 tablespoons unsalted butter
4 chopped shallots
4 tablespoons chopped parsley
2 tablespoons poached beef marrow
1 filet steak (about 8 ounces)

Melt the butter in a saucepan and add the shallots, parsley and beef marrow. Cook until the shallots are lightly browned. Broil the steak on one side, then turn it and spread the second side with the sauce mixture. Broil that side until done. Serve hot.

Veal Cutlets, Milanese Style

Cotelettes de veau à la milanaise

Serves 4

4 veal steaks (about 1 ½ pounds)
1 egg, beaten
½ teaspoon salt
½ teaspoon pepper
1 cup dry breadcrumbs
6 tablespoons clarified unsalted butter
4 tomatoes, peeled, seeded and chopped
½ cup beef broth
3 tablespoons butter
4 ounces lean ham, sliced into julienne strips
1 cup sliced mushrooms
4 cups fresh-cooked macaroni or spaghetti
1 cup grated Parmesan or Gruyère cheese

Place the veal steaks between two pieces of brown or parchment paper and beat them with a steak hammer to flatten them out until they are twice their original size. In a shallow bowl, mix the beaten egg with the salt and pepper. Pour the breadcrumbs into another shallow bowl. Heat the clarified butter in a large skillet. When the grease smokes, it is ready. Dip the veal steaks in the beaten egg, then in the breadcrumbs, making sure the coating is even. Place them in the skillet and cook over high heat, first on one side, then on the other, then reduce the heat and allow to cook through. Remove and drain on paper towels.

Make a tomato sauce by cooking the tomatoes in a saucepan with the beef broth and 2 tablespoons of the butter. Do not let it boil. Add the slices of ham. Melt the remaining tablespoon of butter in another saucepan and add the mushrooms. Sauté them until the juice begins to run. Add the mushrooms to the tomato sauce.

Arrange the filets on a serving platter. Pour the sauce over the veal. Serve with pasta, and pass the cheese separately. Serve hot.

Vienna Schnitzel

Escalopes de veau à la viennoise

Serves 4

4 thin veal steaks (about 1 ½ pounds)
1 egg, beaten
½ teaspoon salt
½ teaspoon pepper
5 tablespoons vegetable oil
1 cup dry breadcrumbs
6 tablespoons butter
4 hardboiled eggs, chopped
4 tablespoons chopped parsley
4 lemon wedges

Place the veal steaks between two pieces of brown or parchment paper and beat them with a steak hammer to flatten them out until they are twice their original size. Pour the beaten egg into a shallow bowl. Add the salt and pepper, and a few drops of the oil. Mix well. Pour the breadcrumbs into another shallow bowl. Heat all but 1 tablespoon of the butter and the rest of the oil in a large skillet. When the grease smokes, it is ready. Dip the veal in the beaten egg, then in the breadcrumbs, making sure the coating is even. Place them in the skillet and brown evenly, first on one side, then on the other. Remove and drain on paper towels.

Arrange on a serving platter. Surround with the hard boiled eggs, parsley and lemon wedges. Melt the rest of the butter, and sprinkle it over the veal. Serve hot.

Calves' Liver in Aspic

Foie de veau en aspic

Serves 8

2½ pounds calves' liver
1 cup madeira or port wine
4 cups broth
1 calves' foot
1 cup dry white wine
1 bouquet garni
3 cloves
⅛ teaspoon mixed spice or allspice

Marinate the liver for 2 hours in the madeira or port. Pour the broth into a flameproof casserole and add the calves' foot and dry white wine. Drain the liver and heat the marinade in a saucepan. Reduce it by half, then add it to the casserole. Add the herbs and spices, and bring to a boil.

Preheat the oven to 350°. Place the liver in the boiling liquid. Cover the casserole and transfer it to the oven. Cook for 30 minutes. Remove the liver from the casserole and cool before serving.

Rib Roast with Olives

Côte de boeuf aux olives

Serves 4

½ cup butter
1 tablespoon oil
1 rolled rib roast (about 3 pounds)
12 pearl onions, peeled and trimmed
4 ounces diced bacon
1 bouquet garni
2 garlic cloves
½ teaspoon salt
½ teaspoon pepper
2 cups green olives, rinsed and pitted
2 cups sliced mushrooms (optional)
2 tablespoons flour

Preheat the oven to 350°. Heat half the butter in a deep pot with a tight-fitting lid. Add the oil and brown the beef on both sides. Arrange the onions and bacon around the beef. Add 2 cups warm water, the bouquet garni, and the garlic. Season with the salt and pepper, then cover tightly. Bring to a boil over medium heat, then place the pot in the oven and cook for 2 hours. Add the olives and the mushrooms, if desired, and cook for another 75 minutes. Remove the meat and keep it warm.

Combine the rest of the butter with the flour into a smooth paste. Cut off pieces of the paste and drop them into the cooking liquid, stirring constantly until the sauce is smooth after each addition. When the flour and butter mixture is used up, remove the sauce from the heat. Pour the sauce over the beef in the bowl.

Veal Meatballs

Boulettes de veau

Serves 4

2 tablespoons vegetable oil
2 onions, minced
1 cup Rich Broth (recipe on page 113)
1 slice bread, crusts removed, soaked in milk
1 pound lean ground veal
4 tablespoons chopped parsley
1 egg, beaten
½ teaspoon salt
½ teaspoon pepper
¼ teaspoon grated nutmeg
½ cup flour
2 teaspoons lemon juice

Heat the oil and add the onion. Sauté until transparent but do not allow to brown. Add the broth and reduce slightly over high heat for 10 minutes. Remove from the heat and reserve.

To make the meatballs, squeeze the soaked bread dry and mix with the ground veal, parsley and beaten egg. Season with the salt, pepper, and nutmeg. Shape into balls 1 inch in diameter.

Roll the balls in the flour. Return the sauce to the heat and, when it is boiling, add the meatballs. Simmer them uncovered for 15 minutes. Add the lemon juice just before serving.

Game

Marinated Haunch of Venison

Gigot de chevreuil mariné

Serves 4

1 haunch of venison (about 3 pounds)
8 ounces lean bacon, sliced into strips
½ teaspoon salt
½ teaspoon pepper
4 tablespoons oil

Marinade

4 tablespoons oil
2 tablespoons white wine vinegar
6 carrots, sliced
6 onions, chopped
4 shallots, minced
1 stalk celery, chopped
1 bouquet garni
1 bottle dry white wine

Combine the ingredients of the marinade in a large bowl. Trim the haunch and lard it with the bacon. Season it with salt and pepper, and place it in the marinade. Leave it in the refrigerator for a day or two, no longer, basting it regularly with the liquid. Strain and reserve the marinade.

Preheat the oven to 450°. Pat the haunch dry with paper towels, trim it, and brush it with the oil. Roast the haunch in a roasting pan for 1 hour, turning it several times in the course of cooking. If it is beginning to brown too much, baste it with some of the reserved marinade. As soon as it is well browned all over, reduce the heat to 350° and cook for another 30 minutes.

Remove the meat from the pan and deglaze the cooking juices, by placing the pan on the stove over low heat for 3 minutes, stirring and scraping with a wooden spoon to dislodge any bits stuck to the bottom. Add 1 cup of the reserved marinade and cook for 10 minutes to reduce the sauce. Serve the sauce with the meat.

Opposite: Jean-Pierre was undoubtedly the best shot in the house. Woodcock was traditionally served for Monet's birthday (recipes on this page and page 149).

Casseroled Woodcock

Bécasse à la casserole

Woodcock should be hung for several days in a cool place. It must not be drawn. When it is well-hung it can be plucked without damaging the skin.

Serves 1-2

4 tablespoons unsalted butter
1 woodcock, drawn and trussed
2 shallots, minced
½ cup dry white wine
Juice of 1 lemon

Melt the butter in a skillet. Add the woodcock and sauté over high heat, turning frequently, for 15 minutes. Add the shallots, white wine, and lemon juice. Reduce the heat and cook for another 10 minutes.

Duck with Turnips

Canard aux navets

Serves 4

1 duckling (4 pounds) with giblets
1 teaspoon salt
½ teaspoon pepper
1 tablespoon unsalted butter or duck fat
2 cups broth
2 ½ pounds turnips, parboiled for 10 minutes

Chop the duck liver and gizzard. Season them with half the salt and all the pepper, and place them inside the cavity. Heat the butter, or better still, duck fat, in a flameproof casserole with a lid. When the butter has melted or the fat is smoking, add the duck. Brown it evenly, turning it frequently. When it is browned, cover the casserole, reduce the heat, and cook on low heat for 1 hour.

Add the broth and bring to the boil. Add the turnips; if some are larger than the others, cut them in two or four. Add the rest of the salt and bring the liquid back to the boil. Cover the pot and continue cooking over low heat for 1 hour.

Braised Pigeons

Pigeons forestière

Serves 4

½ cup lard

4 pigeons

4 carrots, sliced

2 cups mushrooms, sliced

2 onions, thinly sliced

2 stalks celery, finely chopped

½ teaspoon salt

½ teaspoon pepper

1 cup Clear Broth (recipe on page 112)

½ cup cognac

Melt the lard in a Dutch oven or flameproof casserole with a tight-fitting lid. Add the pigeons and sauté them until they are golden-brown all over. Remove them and keep them warm. Sauté the carrots, mushrooms, onions, and celery until they are soft. Mix well and remove half of them from the pot. Return the pigeons to the pot and cover them with the reserved vegetables. Season with the salt and pepper, and sprinkle with the meat cooking juices and cognac. Seal the casserole with a strip of pastry around the lid. Cook over low heat for about 1½ hours. Serve in the casserole.

Pigeon Stew

Pigeons en compote

Serves 4

2 pigeons

4 ounces lean slab bacon, rind removed, diced

4 tablespoons unsalted butter

10 pearl onions

3 cups sliced mushrooms

2 tablespoons flour

2 cups broth

2 cups white Bordeaux wine

½ teaspoon salt

Trim and truss the birds. Blanch the bacon in boiling water for 5 minutes. Drain well. Melt half the butter in a pan just large enough to hold the pigeons, and sauté

the bacon until well-browned. Remove the bacon, and add the onions to the pan ; shake the pan while sautéeing, but do not touch the onions. Remove them and add them to the reserved bacon. Add the mushrooms to the pan. When they are soft, put them with the bacon and onions. Add the pigeons and sauté them until they are lightly browned. Remove and reserve them.

Preheat the oven to 300°. Melt the rest of the butter in the pan and stir in the flour. When the mixture is smooth, add the broth and wine. As soon as the liquid begins to boil, return the pigeons to the pan, and arrange the onions, bacon, and mushrooms around them. Sprinkle with salt. Cover and seal the pot with a strip of pastry around the lid; cook in the oven for 2 hours.

Rabbit Pâté

Potine de lapin

Serves 4

6 slices lean bacon

1 rabbit, cut into 8 pieces

1 teaspoon salt

1 teaspoon pepper

1 large slice fatback or blanched, rinsed salt pork

2−3 onions, thinly sliced

1 bayleaf

1 sprig thyme

10 juniper berries

2 tablespoons brandy

2 cups meat cooking juices or Rich Broth (recipe on page 113)

Preheat the oven to 350°. Arrange half the slices of lean bacon in the bottom of a casserole with a lid. Arrange the pieces of rabbit on top, seasoning each piece with salt and pepper. Slice the rest of the lean bacon into thin strips and cover with the slice of fat . Add the onions, bayleaf, thyme, and juniper berries. Sprinkle with the brandy.

Cover the pot; seal it with a piece of cheesecloth dipped in flour-and-water paste if the lid does not fit tightly. Bake for 1¾ hours. Add the meat cooking juices. Remove the dish from the oven and degrease it while still hot. To do this, turn out the meat onto a perforated board and retain the juice. Degrease it, by allowing it to cool to room temperature, then lifting off the surface grease with paper towels. Return the juice to the pot, discarding the fat and adding the meat. Discard the bayleaf. Leave the contents of the casserole to come to room temperature. Refrigerate until the aspic is set. Serve the rabbit pâté cold.

Duck in Red Wine Sauce
Canard à la rouennaise

Serves 4

1 duckling (4 pounds) with giblets
1 thick slice bacon
4-6 onions
1 teaspoon salt
1 teaspoon pepper
¼ teaspoon mixed spice
4 shallots, chopped
2 cups red wine
2 tablespoons unsalted butter

The duck should be smothered to kill it, so that it loses none of its blood. Preheat the oven to 450°. Trim the bird and remove its innards. Grind the liver with the bacon and onions. Season the mixture, and use it to stuff the bird, then truss it.

Roast the bird for about 30 minutes, depending on how plump it is. It should be lightly browned. Remove it from the oven and cut it into serving pieces, reserving the thighs and wings.

Grease an ovenproof dish and sprinkle with the stuffing mixture and the shallots. Arrange the duck breast fillets on top. Crush the carcass in a mortar to extract all the blood. Mix the blood with the wine and pour it over the breast. Reduce the oven temperature to 300°. Roast the breast for 20 minutes, so that the sauce thickens but do not let the meat cook too thoroughly or it will lose its delicate flavor. While the breast is cooking, melt the butter in a skillet and sauté the thighs and wings until they are evenly browned.

Partridge with Cabbage
Perdrix aux choux

Serves 4

2 partridges, plucked, drawn, singed and trussed
½ cup lard
1 green cabbage, leaves blanched for 10 minutes
1 slice fatback or blanched and rinsed salt pork
3 carrots, sliced
2 small onions, sliced
8 ounces lean bacon, diced
1 pork boiling sausage
2 cups broth
1 tablespoon unsalted butter or lard, cut into pieces

Brown the partridges evenly all over in the lard. Place the fatback in a deep flameproof casserole with a lid, and arrange half the cabbage leaves on top of it. Add the lean bacon and the sausage. Sprinkle with the broth and dot with the butter or lard. Cover the pot and seal it with a strip of cheesecloth dipped in a flour-and-water paste. Cook over medium heat for 2 hours, longer if the birds are not young. If the cooking liquid is too thin, remove the meat and vegetables and reduce it over high heat, uncovered, for 10 minutes. Serve the partridges hot with the sauce in a sauceboat.

Roast Woodcock
Bécasse rotie

Serves 1-2

1 woodcock
1 thin slice fatback or blanched, rinsed salt pork
2 slices day-old bread, fried
½ teaspoon salt

Woodcock is not drawn, except for the gizzard which is removed through a slit made in the neck. The eyes are discarded. Singe the woodcock to remove remaining feathers. Bard it with the fat, then truss the bird well, bending the neck around. Preheat the oven to 450°. Place the bird on the fried bread in an ovenproof dish. Roast for 20 minutes. Sprinkle with salt. Untruss, remove the fat and serve hot with the bread.

Venison with Rosehips

Chevreuil aux cynorhodons

Serves 4

3 pounds boneless venison in one piece
1 cup red wine vinegar
2 teaspoons coarse salt
6 peppercorns
1 slice fatback or blanched, rinsed salt pork
2 cups rosehips
About 2 cups dry white wine
2 tablespoons unsalted butter
2 tablespooons flour
2½ cups slivered almonds
4 cloves
1 seeded lemon, chopped
2 teaspoons sugar

Marinate the venison in the vinegar and 2 cups water, to cover, then season with coarse salt and peppercorns. Leave for at least 2 hours, preferably overnight, in a cool place or the refrigerator.

Preheat the oven to 350°. Grease a roasting pan and pour the marinade into it. Cover the venison with the fat, place it in the roasting pan and roast until tender. The cooking time will vary according to the age of the venison, but should be about 1½ hours. Baste occasionally with the marinade.

Clean the rosehips by trimming, washing and drying them. Split them in half and remove the seeds and hairs in the center. Grind the rosehips and weigh them. Add the same weight of white wine to them. Put them in a soup kettle or heavy-based pan and cook for 35 minutes with ½ cup of the venison cooking juices. Strain the sauce.

In a saucepan, melt the butter and stir in the flour. Add about ½ cup of the venison cooking liquid and the strained sauce. Stir well. Add the almonds, cloves, lemon, and sugar. Stir until the sauce is thickened.

Serve either coated with the sauce or separately.

Duck Pie

Pâté de canard

Serves 8

1 duck (about 5 pounds)
1 ½ pounds boneless lean veal
1 cup dry white wine
3 tablespoons cognac
⅓ pound ground sausage
⅓ cup dry breadcrumbs
1 slice bacon
½ pound savory pic pastry dough
½ cup meat juices or consommé

Bone and skin the duck. Cut the breast and thigh flesh into long strips. Do the same with the veal. Marinate for at least 2 hours in the wine and cognac.

Trim off the rest of the meat from the duck bones, grind it, and mix it with the breadcrumbs and ground sausage. Roll out half the dough and use it to line the bottom and sides of a deep 8-inch pie pan. Cover it with a layer of the sausage mixture. Arrange a layer of duck and veal meat over this. Continue until all are used up. Pat down and cover with the slice of bacon.

Preheat the oven to 400°. Roll out the rest of the dough and use it to cover the pie. Make a small hole in the center and pour the meat juices through it. Lightly cover the pie with parchment paper and bake the pie for 2 ½ hours. Remove the paper and bake for a further 30 minutes. Serve cold.

Opposite: The recipe for venison with rosehips (see above) carefully recorded in one of the journals.

× Sanglier ou chevreuil à la sauce
aux fruits d'églantiers.

——————

Mettre la viande dans deux tiers d'eau
et un tiers de vinaigre, poivre et sel;
et faire cuire jusqu'à ce que la viande
devienne tendre.

Pour faire la sauce mettre, pour trois
livres de viande un demi litre de fruits
d'églantier qu'on a d'abord nettoyés,
lavés et séchés; les piler dans un mortier
et les mettre ensuite dans un pot avec
la même quantité de vin blanc
que de fruits et faire cuire le tout pendant une demi heure en y ajoutant un
peu du jus de la cuisson de la viande,
puis passer au tamis. Ensuite on
fait un petit roux, bien revenu, auquel
on mélange ½ du jus de la cuisson de
la viande et la sauce faite avec les
fruits.

Prendre un quart d'amandes douces
rapées; un zeste d'un demi citron haché menu,
des clous de girofle et un morceau sucre

Fish

Mussels with Fresh Herbs

Moules au vert

Serves 4

48 large mussels (about 5 pints)
4 tablespoons unsalted butter
2 onions, coarsely chopped
4 sprigs parsley
1 teaspoon coarse salt
1 teaspoon black pepper
2 stalks celery
1 cup chervil
4 cups sorrel
½ cup chopped parsley
2 tablespoons chopped tarragon
½ cup dry white wine
½ cup broth
1 tablespoon cornstarch

Wash the mussels well in lots of cold water. Discard any that are not tightly closed or that are broken. Put them in a deep pot with half the butter, the onion, parsley sprigs, salt and pepper, and celery. Cover and cook over high heat for about 10 minutes, shaking the pot vigorously from time to time, until the shells open. Discard any that are still closed. Drain the mussels in a colander, reserving the cooking liquid.

In a skillet, melt the rest of the butter, and add the chervil, sorrel, parsley, and tarragon. Add the cooking liquid from the mussels and the white wine. Add the broth and flour, stirring until smooth. Reheat the mussels in the sauce. If desired, the mussels may be shelled before serving.

Opposite: Despite the difficulties of finding them, fish and crustaceans were often served at Alice's table. Here are mussels with fresh herbs (recipe on this page).

Marinated Fried Sole

Filets de sole à la Horly

Filets of whiting can be substituted for the sole here.

Serves 4

2 cups vegetable oil
Juice of 1 lemon
4 tablespoons chopped parsley
1 onion, thinly sliced
4 filets of sole, skinned
½ teaspoon salt
½ teaspoon pepper
1 cup flour

Prepare a marinade from half the oil, the lemon juice, parsley, and onion. Place the fish in the marinade, and season it with the salt and pepper. Leave for 2 hours.

Drain the fish and dip it in the flour. Heat the rest of the oil in a skillet, and when it smokes, fry the fish until it is well browned.

Oyster Soup

Potage aux huîtres

Serves 6

3 dozen oysters
1 cup court-bouillon (see recipe on page 154) or broth
1 cup madeira wine
4 peppercorns

Poach the oysters in their own water, plus 2 cups fresh water. When they are cooked, after about 10 minutes, reserve 1 oyster per person and remove the rest from the shells. Reserve the cooking liquid and chop the remaining oysters finely. Strain the cooking liquid and add it to the chopped oysters. Add the court-bouillon or chicken broth, then add the madeira and peppercorns. Pour this mixture into a soup kettle or large pan and bring to a boil, uncovered, for 10 minutes to allow it to reduce slightly. To serve, place a whole oyster on the shell in each bowl before pouring the soup into it.

Sole in Shellfish Sauce

Soles à la normande

Serves 8

2 dozen oysters, shucked, liquid reserved
3 dozen small shrimp
1 cup dry white wine
2 dozen mussels
2 dover or lemon soles (about 2 pounds), cleaned, gutted, and trimmed
6 tablespoons unsalted butter
2 tablespoons flour
2 egg yolks
2 tablespoons heavy cream or crème fraîche
Juice of ½ lemon
½ teaspoon salt
½ teaspoon pepper
Slices of truffles poached in madeira

Court-bouillon

4 tablespoons Calvados
2 cups dry white wine
1 leek, white part only, sliced
1 carrot, split in half
1 large onion, thinly sliced
1 whole garlic clove
1 bouquet garni
1 teaspoon coarse salt
5 peppercorns

Put all the court-bouillon ingredients into a pan. Add 2 cups water and bring to a boil. Cover and simmer for 30 minutes. Strain through a conical sieve.

Poach the oysters in their own liquid, covered, for 5 minutes. Retain the cooking liquid and keep the oysters warm. Poach the shrimp in the court-bouillon for 10 minutes. Drain the shrimp, keep them warm, and retain the cooking liquid. Wash the mussels well in lots of cold water, discarding any that are broken or not tightly closed. Pour the white wine into a pan and add the mussels. Cover them tightly and cook, shaking the pan vigorously, over high heat for 5 minutes, or until they are all opened. Discard any that are still closed. Combine the cooking liquid with the liquid from the court bouillon and reserve the mussels.

Preheat the oven to 400°. Heavily grease an ovenproof dish and place the soles in it. Cover them with some of the cooking liquid and with greased parchment paper. Cook for 20 minutes. Meanwhile, combine 2 tablespoons of the butter with the flour. Put it into a saucepan and add 1 ¼ cups of the fish cooking liquid. Stir constantly until smooth. Remove from the heat and cool for 10 minutes. Beat in the egg yolks and cream, beating constantly. Return the sauce to a low heat and, still beating, add the rest of the butter, in small pieces, and the lemon juice. Season with the salt and pepper and continue beating until the liquid is smooth.

Arrange the reserved shellfish around the soles in the ovenproof dish. Coat with the sauce and decorate with the poached truffles.

Fish Soup

Soupe aux poissons

Serves 6

2 leeks, white parts only, sliced lengthwise
3 carrots, split lengthwise
4 onions, quartered
1 teaspoon salt
1 teaspoon pepper
2 ½ pounds mixed fish
2 egg yolks, beaten
2 cups fried croutons

Put the leeks, carrots, and onions into a soup kettle or large pan and add 4 quarts water. Bring to a boil, then simmer for 1½ hours. Season with the salt and pepper and add the fish, cut into serving pieces. Cook over low heat for 20 minutes, then remove the most presentable pieces of fish and keep them warm. Remove the pot from the heat and let the liquid cool for 10 minutes. Add the beaten egg yolks, and stir well. Strain the liquid. Grind the fish which remained in the pot and add them to the strained liquid. Return the soup to the heat to warm it, but do not let it boil. Arrange the pieces of fish in the bowls and pour the soup over them. Garnish with the croutons.

Lobster American-Style
Homard à l'américaine
Serves 4

1 large, live lobster (about 2 ½ pounds)
3 tablespoons vegetable oil
1 teaspoon salt
1 teaspoon pepper
¾ cup unsalted butter
1 onion, finely chopped
3 shallots, chopped
1 garlic clove, crushed
½ cup cognac
2 cups dry white wine
1/8 teaspoon cayenne pepper
2 tablespoons broth

Chop the lobster into serving pieces. Remove the claws. Separate the body from the tail, retaining the liquid which runs out. Cut the body into two parts, and slice the tail into sections. Reserve the coral and the intestines. Pass them through a sieve.

Heat the oil to boiling in a skillet and sauté the lobster flesh in it. Season with half the salt and pepper. Cook for 5 minutes, then remove the lobster and discard the oil it has been cooked in.

Heat 3 tablespoons of the butter in the skillet and put the pieces of lobster back into it along with the onion, shallots, and garlic.

Warm the cognac and flame it before adding it to the pan. Add the wine, salt and pepper, and the cayenne pepper. As soon as the liquid starts to bubble, cover the skillet and simmer for 20 minutes. Remove the lobster pieces and keep them warm.

Boil the sauce over high heat, uncovered, to reduce it. Add the reserved liquid from the body, along with the coral and the intestines. Stir in 2 tablespoons of the butter, and add 2 tablespoons broth, stirring constantly. Remove the skillet from the heat and continue stirring and adding more pieces of butter, stirring well after each addition.

Pour the sauce over the warm lobster and serve the dish immediately.

Brill Dugléré-Style
Barbue à la Dugléré
Serves 6

2 onions, sliced
4-6 medium-size tomatoes, peeled, seeded and crushed
2 shallots, sliced
2 sprigs parsley
1 sprig thyme
1 bayleaf
1 large brill (about 4 pounds), cleaned, gutted and descaled
½ teaspoon salt
½ teaspoon pepper
1 cup dry white wine
1 cup fish broth
2 tablespoons unsalted butter, cut into pieces

Preheat the oven to 400°. Grease a deep ovenproof dish large enough to hold the fish. Cover the bottom with the onions, tomatoes, and shallots. Tie the parsley, thyme and bayleaf in a piece of cheesecloth to make a bouquet garni. Add the bouquet garni to the dish and lay the fish on this bed. Season with the salt and pepper. Moisten with the wine and fish broth. Bring to a boil, cover with greased parchment paper, and transfer it to the oven. Bake for 20 minutes, then remove the dish from the oven but do not turn the oven off.

Carefully pour the sauce into a bowl. Strain it, and pour it into a saucepan. Cook over medium heat, stirring constantly, adding the butter a piece at a time, and stirring well after each addition. When the sauce is smooth and thick, pour it over the brill. Return the dish to the oven and reheat for 5 minutes. Serve in the dish.

Oysters with Sausages
Huîtres aux saucisses

When serving oysters, serve very hot, broiled cocktail sausages at the same time. The two are eaten together and complement each other nicely.

Mackerel in Maître d'Hotel Sauce

Filets de maquereaux à la flamande

Serves 4

4 mackerel filets
2 eggs, beaten
½ cup flour
½ cup unsalted butter

Maître d'Hotel Sauce

2 tablespoons unsalted butter
2 tablespoons flour
4 tablespoons chopped parsley
2 green onions, finely chopped
½ teaspoon salt
½ teaspoon pepper
1/8 teaspoon grated nutmeg
Juice of ½ lemon

Melt ½ cup butter in a skillet. Dip the mackerel in the beaten egg then dust with the flour. Fry the mackerel until evenly browned. Keep warm.

To make the sauce, melt 2 tablespoons of the butter in a saucepan and add the flour. Cook, stirring over low heat, until the butter has absorbed all the flour. Add the parsley and green onions, ½ cup water, salt, pepper, and nutmeg. Stir until the sauce is smooth and thickened. Add the lemon juice at the last moment.

Lobster Newburg

Homard à la Newburg

Serves 4

2 small (1 pound) lobsters
2 quarts court-bouillon (recipe on page 157)
½ cup unsalted butter
1 teaspoon salt
1 teaspoon pepper
1 cup madeira wine
2 cups heavy cream
4 egg yolks

In a large pot, bring the court-bouillon to the boil. Plunge the lobster into the boiling liquid. Cover the pot and cook over very low heat for about 25 minutes. Let the lobster cool in the liquid. When it is cold, split it open and remove the flesh from the shell. Cut it into bite-size pieces.

Melt the butter in a skillet that has a lid and add the pieces of lobster. Season with the salt and pepper. Heat gently for 5 minutes on each side, then add the madeira. Cover and simmer for 15 minutes. Beat the cream with the egg yolks. Beat this into the liquid in the skillet, stirring until the sauce thickens. Stop stirring and cook for 5 minutes without allowing it to boil. Serve hot.

Monkfish American-Style

Baudroie à l'américaine

If the cooked fish steaks are sprinkled with 2 tablespoons of cognac or Armagnac and flamed, the sauce will be even more delicious.

Serves 4

4 monkfish steaks (about 2 pounds)
1 cup flour
1 cup vegetable oil
4 shallots, minced
1 bouquet garni
¼ teaspoon chili pepper
2 cups dry white wine
½ teaspoon salt
½ teaspoon pepper
2 tablespoons tomato paste
½ cup madeira wine
4 cups freshly-cooked long grain rice

Wipe the fish steaks and dust them with the flour. Heat the oil in a skillet and brown them on both sides. Drain off the oil. Add the shallots, bouquet garni, chili pepper, and white wine to the pan. Season with the salt and pepper. Cover and simmer for 15 minutes.

Dilute the tomato paste with 1 cup of the cooking liquid. Add this to the skillet with the madeira. Cook for another 5 minutes. Serve the fish surrounded by the rice and sprinkled with the sauce.

Salt Water Fish Broth

Eau de sel pour la cuisson des poissons

Makes 3 quarts

3 tablespoons coarse salt

This salt water broth, also known in French as "bonne eau," or good water, is used for poaching some types of fish. Catfish, brill, and turbot, among others, are cooked in this way.

Place 3 quarts water in a fish kettle or pan large enough to hold the fish. There should be enough water to cover the fish completely. Add the salt then bring the water to a boil. Reduce the heat and place the fish in the liquid, which should merely tremble, not boil. Cooking time, depending on the weight of the fish, is about 20 minutes per pound.

How to Cook Shrimp and Crab

Cuisson des crevettes et des crabes

Salt the water with sea-salt, then add whole peppercorns, and small quantities of parsley, thyme and bayleaf. Bring the water to a boil and plunge the shrimp or crab into it. Shrimp is cooked from 2 to 4 minutes, crab from 5 to 15 minutes, depending on size. Serve the shellfish warm.

Pike in White Butter Sauce

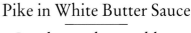

Brochet au beurre blanc

Serves 6–8

1 pike (about 3 pounds), cleaned and gutted, scales left on

Court-Bouillon

4 cups white wine
2 onions, sliced
2 carrots, sliced into rings
1 bouquet garni
1 teaspoon salt

White Butter Sauce

½ cup unsalted butter
2 shallots, chopped
1 teaspoon vinegar
½ teaspoon salt
½ teaspoon pepper

Pour all the court-bouillon ingredients into a fish-kettle with 2 quarts water. Simmer, covered, for 30 minutes. Remove it from the heat and cool to room temperature. Place the pike in the court-bouillon and bring it back to a boil, covered. Then reduce the heat and leave it half off the heat source, so that the water barely moves. If the liquid boils, the flesh will disintegrate. Cook the fish for 30 minutes, or 10 minutes per pound.

When the fish is almost cooked, prepare the white butter sauce. Melt the butter in a saucepan with the shallots, vinegar, salt, and pepper. Stir over low heat until the butter has melted (the sauce must not be allowed to boil) and serve in a heated sauceboat. Lay the fish on a folded napkin to serve.

Pages 158-159: A pike like this would have been gently poached in a court-bouillon and served with white butter sauce (recipe on this page).

Lobster Douglas

Homard à la Douglas

Cooked mushrooms and/or truffles could be used to garnish this dish.

Serves 4

1 large live lobster (about 2 ½ pounds)
1 ½ cups unsalted butter
½ teaspoon salt
½ teaspoon cayenne pepper
½ cup gin
2 tablespoons heavy cream or crème fraîche
1 tablespoon flour

Court-Bouillon

2 onions, each studded with 1 clove
5 peppercorns
1 large carrot
1 tablespoon coarse salt
2 sprigs thyme
1 bayleaf

Mirepoix

2 carrots, thinly sliced
2 onions, chopped
½ teaspoon dried thyme
1 bayleaf

In a large pot, combine the ingredients for the court-bouillon with 2 quarts water and bring them to a boil. Plunge the lobster into the boiling liquid. Cover the pot and cook over reduced heat for about 25 minutes. Let the lobster cool in the liquid. When it is cold, remove the flesh from the shell. Cut it into bite-size pieces.

Place the shell and the coral in a mortar and grind it with 1¼ cups of the butter. Cook the mixture over low heat with 2 quarts cold water. Bring it to a boil, and simmer over very low heat for 15 minutes. Remove the pot from the heat and cool to room temperature, then chill in the refrigerator, so that the lobster butter rises to the surface. Skim off the butter and place it in a strainer.

Place ½ cup of the lobster butter in a deep skillet. Melt it and add the mirepoix mixture. Cook over low heat for 15 minutes, or until the vegetables are lightly colored. Place the pieces of lobster over the mixture. Season with the salt and cayenne pepper. Turn the meat over, sprinkle it with the gin and flame it. Moisten with the cream, while stirring. Continue to stir until the liquid boils, then add the rest of the lobster butter. Stir and cook until the butter is incorporated. Combine the rest of the fresh butter with the flour to make a paste. Carefully add this paste, in several pieces, to the sauce, stirring constantly after each addition. Pour the sauce under and over the lobster and serve.

Salt Cod Croquettes

Croquettes de morue

Serves 4

1 pound salt cod
About 1 quart milk or water
5 potatoes, peeled
3 eggs, beaten
2 cups vegetable oil
½ cup flour

Béchamel Sauce

2 ½ tablespoons flour
2 ½ tablespoons unsalted butter
½ cup milk, scalded

Place the salt cod in a colander, skin side up and soak it in water for 24 hours to remove the salt, changing the water occasionally. Place the cod in the milk or water and bring to a boil. Reduce the heat until the liquid barely moves and cover the pan. Cook for 15 minutes.

Boil the potatoes in water to cover. Drain them and mash them. Remove the cod from the pan and purée it while it is still hot. Combine the potatoes and the cod.

Make the sauce by combining the flour and butter in a saucepan. Stir until they are smooth, then add the milk all at once. Stir until it is smooth and thick.

Stir the sauce into the potato and cod mixture, and add 2 of the beaten eggs. Heat the oil in a skillet. Shape the mixture into croquettes. Roll them in the flour, dip them in the remaining beaten egg and deep-fry the croquettes until they are golden. Serve very hot.

Florentine Filets of Sole

Filets de sole à la florentine

Serves 4

1 quart court-bouillon (recipe on page 154)
4 filets of sole
2 cups fresh spinach
1 cup thick Béchamel Sauce (recipe on page 160)
½ cup grated Gruyère cheese

Pour the court-bouillon into a fish kettle and poach the sole filets in it for 15 minutes. Remove and drain them. In a saucepan, cook the spinach in its own liquid until it wilts. Drain and squeeze to remove excess moisture. Arrange the spinach in a greased, ovenproof dish and lay the sole fillets on top. Preheat the oven to 450°. Pour the Béchamel Sauce over the fish and sprinkle with the grated cheese. Bake for 10 minutes or until the cheese melts and bubbles. Serve very hot, or the sauce will separate.

Fish Creole

Poisson à la créole

Serves 6

6 cod steaks (about 3 pounds)
3 teaspoons salt
½ teaspoon pepper
Juice of 1 lemon
½ cup unsalted butter
1 hot red chili pepper, seeded and chopped
1 bouquet garni
5 cups long grain rice
2 tablespoons tomato paste
1 egg yolk

Soak the cod steaks in water to cover with 1 teaspoon of the salt and the lemon juice for 2 hours. Drain and pat dry with paper towels. Melt half the butter in a skillet and add the cod steaks. Cover with hot water, then add the chili pepper and bouquet garni. Season with 1 teaspoon of the salt and the pepper. Cover the pan and simmer for 15 minutes. Remove the fish and reserve it.

Rinse the rice and sprinkle it into a deep pot containing 2 ½ quarts boiling water and the rest of the salt. Stir, cover tightly and bring to a boil. Reduce the heat and cook for 15 to 20 minutes.

Dilute the tomato paste with some of the fish cooking liquid. Add to the contents of the skillet and stir to incorporate. Boil uncovered for 20 minutes, or until the liquid is reduced. Bind with the egg yolk when the rice is ready. Do not let the sauce boil.

Preheat the oven to 400°. Pour the rice into a colander and rinse it under cold water, then drain it again. Pile it into a large ovenproof dish and leave it in the oven, stirring the grains from time to time to keep them separate. Place the fish in the center of the dish with the rice surrounding it . Pour the sauce over the dish.

Mixed Fish Stew

Costriade

Serves 6

2 tablespoons unsalted butter
2 onions, chopped
½ teaspoon salt
½ teaspoon pepper
1 bouquet garni
2 garlic cloves
1 pound potatoes, peeled and cut into large pieces
2 pounds mixed fish (hake, mackerel, sardines, conger eel, shrimp, crab, mussels, etc.)

In a large deep pot, melt the butter and sauté the onions. When they are colored, add 2 quarts hot water. Season with salt and pepper. Add the bouquet garni, garlic and potatoes. Bring the water to a boil and boil, covered, for 20 minutes.

Slice the larger fish into pieces, leaving the sardines, shrimps, and mussels whole. Add them to the pot. Reduce the heat and inspect the pot occasionally to make sure the fish do not disintegrate.

Serve the fish and potatoes in a shallow bowl, and serve the broth separately, pouring it over slices of bread placed in soup bowls.

Sole Filets in Véron Sauce

Filets de sole à la Véron

Serves 8

8 filets of sole
⅓ cup melted unsalted butter
4 tablespoons flour

Véron Sauce

2 egg yolks, beaten
1 cup reduced fish broth
4 tablespoons unsalted butter
1 tablespoon heavy cream or crème fraîche
1 cup dry white wine
1 cup white wine vinegar
1 teaspoon chopped tarragon
1 teaspoon chopped chervil
1 teaspoon chopped shallots
½ teaspoon salt
1 cup vegetable oil
1 tablespoon strong beef broth
¼ teaspoon cayenne pepper

To make the sauce, beat the egg yolks into the reduced fish broth. Beat in the butter and cream; reserve.

Pour the white wine into a small saucepan. Add the vinegar and chopped herbs, and season with the salt. Boil until it is reduced by half. Let it cool. Strain the sauce and put it back in the saucepan over low heat. Beat the contents of the pan with a wire whip, gradually adding the oil, and beating well after each addition. When it is used up, beat in the meat glaze, and the reserved fish broth. Sprinkle with the cayenne pepper.

Dip the filets of sole in the melted butter, then in the flour. Broil them under a low heat. When they are lightly browned on both sides, arrange them on a napkin and serve with the Véron Sauce.

Salt Cod Soup (Cézanne's Recipe)

Bouillabaisse de morue (Cézanne)

Serves 6

large piece of salt cod (about 1 pound)
2 cups olive oil
½ cup flour
6 potatoes, sliced
4 leeks, white parts only, sliced crosswise
½ teaspoon pepper
¼ teaspoon ground cloves
2 garlic cloves, minced
2 tablespoons chopped parsley
1/8 teaspoon saffron
1 bayleaf

Place the salt cod in a colander, skin side up and soak it in water for 24 hours to remove the salt, changing the water occasionally. Drain well and pat dry. Heat the olive oil in a skillet. When it is smoking, dust the salt cod with some of the flour and fry it until it is cooked through, but not brown. Remove, drain and reserve it. Sauté the potatoes in the same skillet for about 10 minutes, until they are almost cooked through.

Pour a little of the frying oil into a deep cast-iron pot. Add the leeks and sauté them on low heat. Slowly add the pepper, cloves, garlic, parsley, saffron, bayleaf, and the rest of the flour, which will brown in the oil. Add 6 cups hot water, and boil, covered, over high heat for 10 to 15 minutes. Slide the cod and potatoes into the pot.

Opposite: Recipes from the cooking journals for shoulder of pork contributed by Sacha Guitry (recipe on page 140), and for Cézanne's salt cod soup (recipe on this page).

Palette de porc (sacha)

———

Mettre la palette à cuire dans de l'eau froide quand elle bout on met les choux, les pommes de terre laisser cuire 2 heures ; ajouter le saucisson - laissez cuire 1/2 heure et servez -

———

Bouillabaisse de Morue (cézanne)
faire tremper la morue pour la dessaler - La faire frire ne pas attendre qu'elle soit croustillante. Faire frire à 3/4 de la cuisson des pommes de terre coupées en tranches. Mettre dans une casserole de l'huile dans laquelle on fait revenir des tranches. Avec des poireaux pendant ce temps assaisonner de poivre clous de girofle et persil haché, safran 1 feuille de laurier et faire brunir un peu de farine le tout doit être fait très lentement - Mettre l'eau chaude 1 verre par personne après

oignon pour y faire bien

Desserts

Green Cake

Vert-vert

Serves 8-10

Cake

4 eggs
¾ cup sugar
1 cup flour, sifted
2 tablespoons ground pistachios
4 tablespoons kirsch
2 tablespoons unsalted butter, softened
Grated rind of 1 lemon

Spinach Coloring

3 cups fresh spinach

Pistachio Cream

4 tablespoons ground pistachios
2 tablespoons kirsch
2¼ cups unsalted butter, softened
2 teaspoons spinach coloring (see below)
⅓ cup sugar
2 eggs
2 yolks
2 teaspoons flour
1 cup milk

Fondant Frosting

3 cups sugar
2 tablespoons white corn syrup
1 teaspoon spinach coloring (see below)
Juice of 1 lemon

First make the spinach coloring. Bring ½ cup water to a boil and blanch the spinach in it for 1 minute. Strain the liquid and pass the spinach through a sieve. This will give a green purée to color the pistachio cream and the frosting.

Preheat the oven to 300°. Grease an 8-inch cake pan. To make the cake, place a saucepan over a low heat and break the eggs into it. Beat them with the sugar until the mixture has doubled in volume. Beat in the flour until it is completely incorporated. Add the pistachios, kirsch, softened butter, and lemon rind. Stir well with a wooden spoon or spatula. Pour the mixture into the cake pan and bake for 30 minutes. Test with a knife to see if the cake is done. If so, remove it from the oven, turn it upside down on a wire rack and let it cool.

To make the pistachio cream, combine the pistachios, kirsch and 2 tablespoons of the softened butter into a smooth paste. Color it with the spinach coloring. In a saucepan off the heat, combine the sugar with the whole eggs and the yolks. Beat in the flour and milk, stirring constantly. Heat this mixture over a low heat, stirring, and beat in the pistachio paste. Remove the mixture from the heat and beat in the rest of the softened butter.

Carefully slice the cake into three equal layers. Spread two of the rounds with the pistachio cream, then stack the layers together again. Refrigerate.

To make the fondant frosting, dissolve the sugar in a heavy pan with 2 cups water. Heat, without stirring, over high heat until the sugar dissolves and begins to boil. Check the syrup cooking stage while it is boiling. When the syrup reaches the large thread stage (that is, when a little of the syrup is dropped in cold water it forms a large thread), add the corn syrup and the spinach coloring, and remove from the heat.

Lightly oil a marble work surface. Pour the syrup onto the surface and work it with a wooden spatula, until it starts to become opaque. Sprinkle with the lemon juice and continue working until it is a smooth, pale green paste. Roll it into a ball and wrap it in a damp cloth. Refrigerate until needed. Roll it out with a rolling pin and use it to cover the cake.

Opposite: One of Marguerite's specialties was the beautiful green cake called the *vert-vert* (recipe on this page).

Christmas Pudding (a good one)

Christmas pudding (de bonne)

Serves 12

1 pound beef kidney fat (suet), chopped
2 cups flour
12 eggs
1 cup seedless raisins
1 cup currants
2/3 cup confectioner's sugar
Peel of 1 lemon, finely chopped
3/4 cup brandy
1 cup milk
1 cup dry breadcrumbs

Put the fat and flour into a bowl. Break the eggs into it and add the raisins and currants, as well as the sugar, chopped lemon peel, and half the brandy. Mix well with a wooden spoon. Add the milk and breadcrumbs, to make a mixture that is light, smooth but fairly stiff.

Fill a large pot with enough water to cover the pudding and bring it to a boil. Grease and flour a pudding cloth. Place the mixture in it and shape it into a ball. Tie the four corners of the cloth tightly together, leaving room inside for the pudding to expand. Put the pudding in the pot and half-cover it. Boil the pudding on low heat for 5 to 6 hours, adding boiling water from time to time to ensure that the level does not drop. Drain, untie the cloth and turn it out onto a platter, removing the cloth. When ready to serve, warm the rest of the brandy, pour it over the pudding and flame.

Hard Sauce

Sauce pour le pudding

Serves 12

2/3 cup unsalted butter
2 egg yolks
3 tablespoons confectioner's sugar
2 tablespoons rum

Combine the ingredients in a small double boiler. Stir until the mixture thickens and serve it hot.

Baked Peaches

Croûtes aux pêches

Serves 6

6 slices bread, crusts removed
3 ripe peaches, cut in half, pitted
6 tablespoons sugar
1/2 cup unsalted butter, cut into 6 pieces

Preheat the oven to 325°. Generously grease an 8-inch pie pan and arrange the slices of bread in it. Place half a peach, cut side up, on each slice of bread. In the cavity left by the pit, sprinkle 1 tablespoon sugar and 1 piece of butter. Bake for 20 minutes or until cooked through. Serve warm or cold.

Upside Down Apple Tart

Tarte Tatin

Serves 8

2 cups flour
5 tablespoons confectioner's sugar
1/8 teaspoon salt
1 egg yolk
1 cup unsalted butter, cut into pieces
6 dessert apples, peeled and sliced

Pour the flour into a bowl, make a well in the center and in it put half the sugar, the salt, the egg yolk and 1/2 cup warm water. Mix well, then add half the butter. Mix the dough until smooth, then roll it out into a rectangle. Fold up the rectangle, by folding one third toward the center, then folding the remaining third over the top of the folded part. Cover with a damp cloth and let it rest for 1 hour. Roll out the dough again into a circle 1/4 inch thick.

Preheat the oven to 400°. Arrange the apple slices in a deep pie dish. Add the rest of the pieces of butter, and sprinkle with the rest of the sugar. Cover with the dough. Bake for 45 minutes. Turn the tart out onto a plate so that the pastry is on top.

Pound Cake

Quatre-quarts

The French name for this cake means Four Quarters, because it uses equal quantities (by weight) of eggs, butter, sugar, and flour.

Serves 8

5 eggs, separated
About ⅔ cup unsalted butter
About ⅔ cup sugar
About 1 ¼ cups flour
1 teaspoon grated lemon rind

Preheat the oven to 325°. Grease a deep 8-inch cake pan. Weigh the eggs and weigh out the same weight of butter, sugar and flour. Melt the butter in a saucepan. When it begins to melt, remove it from the heat. Beat the egg yolks with the sugar in a bowl with the grated rind. When the mixture turns pale, add the melted butter. Mix well. Gradually beat in the flour. Beat the egg whites into peaks. When the mixture is smooth, incorporate the egg whites, folding them in gently. Pour the mixture into the prepared cake pan and bake for 1 hour.

Mélanie's Puff Pastry Cheesecake

Galette feuilletée (Mélanie)

Serves 8

2 cups flour
½ teaspoon salt
½ cup unsalted butter, softened
½ cup cream cheese, at room temperature
1 egg, beaten

Sift the flour into a bowl. Make a well in the center and pour 4 tablespoons warm water, and the salt, into it. Gradually incorporate the water and salt into the flour to make a dough. Knead the dough into a ball. Cover with a damp cloth and let it rest for 30 minutes. Beat the softened butter and the cheese together.

Roll out the dough into a rectangle about ¼ inch thick. Place the butter and cheese mixture in the center

and fold the dough over it. Roll over it with the rolling pin several times, then fold the dough in half and in half again. Give it a quarter turn and roll it out again. Repeat, giving the dough another quarter turn, then let it rest for 15 minutes. Do this a total of eight times, giving it 6 quarter turns.

Preheat the oven to 375°. Roll the dough out to fit a round pie pan. It should be about the thickness of a finger. Bake for 30 minutes or until golden.

Soufflé Fritters (Mélanie's Recipe)

Beignets soufflés ou Pets-de-nonne (Mélanie)

Makes about 12

1 cup milk
1/8 teaspoon salt
¼ teaspoon sugar
½ cup unsalted butter
1 tablespoon brandy
1 cup flour
4 eggs
2 cups vegetable oil
1 cup confectioner's sugar, sifted

Heat the milk in a saucepan with the salt, sugar, butter, and brandy. As soon as the liquid boils, add the flour. Put the pan on the side of the heat source and beat the mixture well with a wooden spoon until it is smooth and starts to leave the sides of the pan without sticking to the spoon. Remove the pan from the heat and break the eggs into it, beating until smooth after adding each egg. The dough should be soft but not liquid.

Leave the dough to rest for 1 hour. Heat the oil in a deep skillet. Shape the dough into small balls and deep-fry them in the skillet. Increase the heat as the fritters swell up. When they are nicely puffed up and browned, remove them with a skimmer, drain them on paper towels and transfer them to a platter. When all are cooked sprinkle them with the confectioner's sugar.

Chocolate Gâteau

Gâteau au chocolat

This recipe uses equal quantities by weight of eggs, butter, chocolate, and sugar, so these ingredients will have to be weighed to find out the exact amount to use.

Serves 8

2 eggs, separated
About 4 tablespoons unsalted butter
About 2 ounces semisweet chocolate
About ½ cup confectioner's sugar
2 tablespoons flour

Weigh the eggs. Weigh out an equal amount of butter, chocolate and confectioner's sugar. Melt the chocolate in a small pan with 2 tablespoons water. Remove from the heat and beat in the butter. When the mixture is smooth let it cool. Preheat the oven to 325°. Beat the yolks and stir them into the mixture. Then beat in the confectioner's sugar and the flour. Beat the egg whites into stiff peaks and fold them into the mixture. Pour the mixture into a well-greased cake pan and bake for 20 minutes.

Chocolate Square

Pavé au chocolat

Serves 6

8 ounces semisweet chocolate
½ cup unsalted butter
1 egg
12 sugared sponge cakes, split in half horizontally

Melt the chocolate over very low heat with 3 tablespoons water. Stir it and when it is completely smooth, beat in the butter. Beat the whole egg and stir it into the mixture. Have a pan of warm water ready on the stove.

Place 12 cake halves in a dish, cut side up. Spread some of the chocolate mixture on the cut sides, then cover with the other half.

Arrange three of the cakes lengthwise close together on a serving dish. Cover them with chocolate mixture.

Then arrange three more cakes crosswise next to them. Cover them with more chocolate mixture. Add the next three below the crosswise cakes but arrange them lengthwise; spread them with the mixture. Add the last three to complete the square. Spread the square with the rest of the chocolate mixture. Smooth it with a warmed metal spatula. If the cream becomes too stiff to spread while you are working, dip the bowl in the pan of warm water over the heat.

Strawberry mousse

Mousse aux fraises

Serves 4

2 cups strawberries
½ cup confectioner's sugar
4 egg whites

Pass the strawberries through a sieve. Mix the strawberry juice with the confectioner's sugar. Preheat the oven to 300°. Grease an 8-inch pie pan. Beat the egg whites into very stiff peaks and carefully fold the strawberry juice into them. Pour the mixture into the pan and bake for 10 minutes. Serve immediately.

Mocha Cream

Crème moka

Serves 4

6 egg yolks
2 cups flour
1 cup sugar
1 cup unsalted butter, softened
About 1 cup strong black coffee

Beat the yolks in a bowl with the flour, sugar and softened butter. Pour in the coffee, beating constantly. When the coffee no longer mixes into the cream, stop pouring. Cook the mixture, stirring constantly with a wooden spoon, for 10 minutes on low heat.

Vanilla Cream

Crème à la vanille

Serves 4

4 cups milk
1-inch piece vanilla bean
1 cup sugar
6 egg yolks
2 eggs

Preheat the oven to 300°. Boil the milk with the vanilla bean and sugar for 10 minutes. Remove the milk from the heat and cool slightly before beating in the egg yolks and whole eggs. Beat with a wire whip. Strain the mixture through a fine sieve and pour it into a baking dish. Place the baking dish in a large roasting pan half-filled with water. Bake for 30 minutes, or until set.

Chestnut Cake

Gâteau de marrons

Serves 12

1 quart milk
1 cup sugar
1 vanilla bean
3 pounds peeled chestnuts
¾ cup unsalted butter, softened
6 eggs, separated

Grease a charlotte mold. Heat the milk with the sugar and vanilla bean. Stir until the sugar has dissolved, then bring to a boil. Add the chestnuts and cook for about 30 minutes, or until they are soft. Remove and drain them. Discard the vanilla bean. Pass the chestnuts through a sieve then beat the butter into the chestnuts. When the purée has cooled to lukewarm, stir in the egg yolks, one after the other, beating well after each addition.

Preheat the oven to 325°. Beat the egg whites into stiff peaks and fold them into the puree. Pour the mixture into a charlotte mold. Set the mold in a baking pan filled with warm water, and bake for 30 minutes. Remove from the heat and leave to cool. This is eaten cold.

Genoese Sponge

Génoise

Serves 8

3 eggs
2 egg yolks
½ cup sugar
1 cup flour, sifted
½ cup unsalted butter, melted
1 tablespoon rum

Grease an 8-inch cake pan, line it with parchment paper, and grease the paper.

Place the eggs, egg yolks and sugar in a bowl over 2 inches of water barely simmering in a pan, or in a double boiler. Beat them for at least 10 minutes until very thick, light and lukewarm. Remove from the water and continue beating a further five minutes or more, until it leaves a trail on the surface when the beaters are lifted.

Preheat the oven to 350°. Sift a little of the flour into the egg and sugar mixture and fold it in carefully using a metal spoon. Gradually add the rest of the flour in the same way, then add the rum, beating until the mixture is smooth. Fold in the melted butter a spoonful at a time.

Pour into the prepared pan and bake for 20-25 minutes or until a knife inserted in the center comes out clean.

Flat Cake

Galette

Serves 8

2 cups flour
2 teaspoons salt
1 cup unsalted butter
½ cup milk
1 egg, beaten

Combine all the ingredients except the egg to form a dough. Sprinkle a work surface with flour and roll out the dough into a rectangle. Fold it over on itself and let it rest, under a damp cloth, for 15 minutes. Do this three times, giving the dough a quarter turn each time, and letting it rest under a damp cloth for 15 minutes.

Roll out the dough into a large circle and lay it on a greased baking sheet. Preheat the oven to 350°. Use a sharp knife to trace a lattice pattern on the dough. Brush the dough with beaten egg. Bake for approximately 30 minutes or until the cake is golden.

Apple Doughnuts

Beignets de pommes

Serves 6

1 cup flour
2 egg yolks
1 tablespoon brandy
¼ teaspoon salt
About ½ cup milk
6 tart dessert apples
2 cups vegetable oil
1 cup sugar

Pour the flour into a bowl and make a well in the center. Into it, put the egg yolks, brandy and salt. Gradually mix in the flour, then add enough milk to make a supple, smooth batter which is fairly thick . Let it rest for at least 20 minutes.

Peel the apples, core and slice them and put them into the batter. Heat the oil in a skillet and deep-fry the apple slices. When cooked, drain and sprinkle with sugar.

Upside Down Cream

Crème renversée

Serves 6

1 quart milk
2 cups confectioner's sugar
1-inch piece of vanilla bean
6 eggs, beaten

Rinse a mold in cold water. Scald the milk with 1 ½ cups of the sugar and the vanilla bean. Remove from the heat, discard the vanilla bean and leave to cool. Beat the eggs into the milk. Make a caramel by melting the rest of the sugar with 2 tablespoons water in a heavy pan and allowing to boil just until it begins to color. Quickly pour it into the mold and turn the mold to coat the bottom and sides evenly. Let it cool, then pour in the egg-and-milk mixture.

Preheat the oven to 350°. Set the mold in a pan half-filled with warm water and place it in the oven. Bake for 30 minutes or until set. Remove and let it cool. When the cream is firm, turn it out onto a dish.

Cream to Accompany Rice Pudding

Crème pour accompagner le pudding au riz

Serves 6

3 tablespoons unsalted butter
3 tablespoons sugar
2 egg yolks, beaten
Juice of ½ lemon
½ cup sherry

In a small saucepan, melt the butter over low heat and stir in the sugar. Add the beaten egg yolks, stirring until the mixture is light and fluffy. Continue beating with a wooden spoon while adding the hot water. Put the saucepan into a larger saucepan containing hot water. Continue to beat with a wire whip, while adding the lemon juice and sherry. Cook for 5 minutes. Serve warm with rice pudding.

Fried Custard

Crème frite

Makes about 10

5 tablespoons flour
1 cup scalded milk
4 eggs
2 tablespoons sugar
1 egg white, lightly beaten
1 cup dry cake crumbs
½ cup vegetable oil or unsalted butter

Combine the flour and scalded milk, beating well. Leave to cool. Beat the eggs and sugar into the dough. Transfer the mixture to a saucepan and cook, stirring with a wooden spoon, for 30 minutes. Pour the dough onto a wetted marble slab and roll it out until it is the thickness of a finger. Let it cool. When cold, cut it into diamonds, rounds, and rectangles.

Heat the oil or butter in a skillet. Dip the custards into the beaten egg white and then into the cake crumbs. Sauté them until they are golden.

Cherry Bake

Clafouti

Reserve the cherry pits for adding to other baked or stewed fruit to give it a good flavor.

Serves 4

1 cup flour
¾ cup confectioner's sugar
2 eggs
1/8 teaspoon salt
1 ¼ cups milk
2 tablespoons unsalted butter
5 cups (1 pound) cherries, pitted

Preheat the oven to 375°. Make a batter with the flour, 2 tablespoons of the sugar, the eggs, salt, and the milk, beating the mixture until smooth. It should not be too liquid. Grease a pie pan and put the cherries into it; they should be tightly packed. Pour the batter over them and sprinkle with the rest of the sugar. Bake for about 45 minutes or until the batter is golden.

Chestnut Soufflé

Soufflé aux marrons

The original recipe recommends baking in a country oven with low heat below and high heat above.

Serves 6

1 pound peeled chestnuts
2 cups milk
1-inch piece vanilla bean
½ cup sugar
3 eggs, separated

Put the chestnuts into a saucepan and add the milk, vanilla bean and sugar. Simmer over low heat, uncovered, for 30 minutes or until the chestnuts are softened. Drain the chestnuts, reserving the cooking liquid. Discard the vanilla bean. Grind the chestnuts. Put them in a bowl and stir in the cooking liquid. When the mixture is smooth beat in the egg yolks, one at a time. Preheat the oven to 350°. Beat the egg whites into stiff peaks, then fold them into the chestnut mixture.

Pour the mixture into a greased soufflé dish. Bake for approximately 30 to 40 minutes or until the soufflé is well risen and lightly colored on top.

Soufflé Omelet

Omelette soufflée

Serves 4

6 eggs, separated
1 ¼ cups sugar
1 teaspoon grated lemon rind
1 tablespoon unsalted butter

Beat the yolks with 6 tablespoons of the sugar and the grated rind. Beat the egg whites into very stiff peaks. When they are stiff, beat in 1 tablespoon sugar.

Preheat the oven to 375°. Fold the whites into the yolks. Melt the butter in an ovenproof dish and pour the mixture into it. Sprinkle the rest of the sugar over the top. Bake for 6 to 8 minutes or until lightly browned. Serve immediately, because the omelet sinks quickly.

Apricot Charlotte

Charlotte aux abricots

Serves 8

2 pounds lady fingers
4 tablespoons kirsch
1 cup apricot jam, warmed

Dip the lady fingers in the kirsch and use them to line the bottom and sides of a charlotte mold. Fill any gaps with broken fingers. Spread with a layer of preserves. Arrange another layer of lady fingers on top of the first, and at right angles to them. Spread with preserves. Continue layering and spreading with preserves until the mold is full. Cover with a tight-fitting lid and place a weight on top of it. Leave in a cool place. Serve with vanilla-flavored custard.

Jelly Roll

Biscuit roulé

Serves 6

½ cup sugar
4 eggs, separated
¾ cup flour
1 tablespoon rum
1 cup apricot jelly

Caramel Glaze

½ cup sugar

Grease a sheet of parchment paper large enough to fit a baking sheet. Preheat the oven to 325°. Beat the sugar with the egg yolks for 10 minutes. Gradually add the flour, then add the rum. Beat the egg whites into stiff peaks. Carefully fold them into the mixture. Turn the mixture out onto the parchment paper. Bake for about 30 minutes, or until the cake begins to take on a golden color.

Remove the cake from the oven and let it cool slightly. Place a cloth over a marble surface and turn the cake out, papered side up, on the cloth. Remove the paper. Spread the jelly evenly over the cake. Use the cloth to help you roll up the cake while it is still hot. Let it cool.

To make the caramel glaze, heat 1 cup water with the sugar in a heavy-based pan. Bring to a boil without stirring and do not stir when boiling. As soon as the syrup begins to color, pour it over the jelly roll, to form a caramel glaze.

Baked Apples

Pommes au beurre

Serves 4

4 slices day-old bread
4 large tart apples, peeled and cored
½ cup unsalted butter
1 cup sugar
4 tablespoons blackcurrant preserves

Preheat the oven to 400°. Grease a shallow baking dish. Cut the bread into circles, the size of the apples. Lay the bread circles on the dish and arrange the apples on the bread. Cut four small pieces of butter and put each one in the hole in the center of the apple. Bake for 10 minutes, then put a teaspoon of sugar into the hole. Bake for another 10 minutes. Combine four tablespoons sugar with four tablespoons butter. Divide in four and fill the holes with the mixture. Bake for another 40 minutes. Just before serving, fill the hole in the centers with the blackcurrant preserves.

Apricot Soufflé

Soufflé à l'abricot

Serves 8

8 egg whites
12-ounce jar apricot preserves

Preheat the oven to 250°. Beat the egg whites into stiff peaks. Gradually fold them into the apricot preserves. Pour into a greased soufflé dish and bake for 1½ hours. If the oven is too hot the soufflé will not rise.

Savoy Sponge

Biscuit de Savoie

Serves 6

6 eggs, separated
¾ cup confectioner's sugar
¾ cup flour, sifted
2 tablespoons unsalted butter

Grease a deep 8-inch cake pan. Preheat the oven to 325°. Beat the egg yolks with the sugar until the mixture turns pale. Gradually beat in the flour. Beat the egg whites into stiff peaks and fold them into the mixture. Bake for about 50 minutes or until a knife inserted into the cake comes out clean.

Stewed Peaches

Pêches à la Bourdaloue

Serves 6

6 large, ripe peaches
1 ½ cups sugar
1 vanilla bean
4 macaroon cookies, crushed
2 tablespoons unsalted butter, cut into pieces

Pastry Cream

6 egg yolks
½ cup sugar
1 tablespoon flour
2 cups milk

Place the peaches in boiling water to blanch them and loosen the skins. Peel them, and cut them in half. Discard the pits. Put the sugar, water, and vanilla bean into a heavy pan and bring to a boil, stirring only until the sugar dissolves. Boil the syrup for 5 minutes then add the peach halves. Remove the pan from the heat, leaving the peaches to soak in the syrup.

Make the pastry cream. Beat the egg yolks with 2 tablespoons of the sugar and the flour. Boil the milk and gradually beat it into the mixture. Transfer the mixture to a saucepan and heat it, stirring constantly. As soon as

it boils, remove it from the heat and let it cool. When it is cold, spread half of it over the bottom of a greased ovenproof dish. Drain the peaches and arrange them on top, then cover with another layer of custard.

Melt the remaining sugar in a dry skillet. As soon as the sugar colors, remove the skillet from the heat and stir in the crushed cookies. When cool, crush this brittle with a rolling pin. Sprinkle the mixture over the custard and dot with the butter.

Preheat the oven to 350°. Bake for about 15 minutes, or until the brittle melts and coats the custard. Serve the stewed peaches warm.

Brioche with Green Plums

Brioches aux reines-claudes

Serves 6

6 slices brioche
4 tablespoons unsalted butter
1 pound green plums (greengages), halved and pitted
½ cup confectioner's sugar

Preheat the oven to 350°. Butter the slices of brioche and arrange them in a buttered ovenproof dish. Cover them with the halved plums, then sprinkle with the confectioner's sugar. Bake for 15 minutes.

Apple Fritters

Pommes frites

Serves 4

4 apples, peeled, cored, and sliced
½ cup brandy
4 tablespoons confectioner's sugar
1 cup flour
½ cup unsalted butter

Marinate the apple slices in the brandy and confectioner's sugar for several hours. Drain them and dip them in flour. Melt the butter in a skillet and sauté the apple slices until golden.

Rich Chocolate Cream

Crème somptueuse

Prepare this delicious chocolate cream 24 hours in advance so that it sets well. It can be kept in the refrigerator for two or three days.

Serves 6

12 ounces semisweet chocolate
½ cup unsalted butter, cut into pieces
3 egg yolks

In a saucepan over very low heat or in a double boiler, dissolve the chocolate in 3 tablespoons water. Stir with a wooden spoon and when the chocolate forms a cream, remove the pan from the heat. Beat in the butter, 1 piece at a time, until the mixture is smooth. Beat the egg yolks in a bowl. Beat in the chocolate mixture gradually with a wooden spoon, until you have a smooth paste. Turn it into a serving bowl.

Burnt Cream

Crème brûlée

Serves 4

1 cup heavy cream or crème fraîche
6 egg yolks
2 tablespoons granulated sugar
4 tablespoons crushed praline or soft brown sugar

Pour the cream into a saucepan and stand it in a larger saucepan of hot water, or in a double boiler. Heat but do not let it boil.

Beat the egg yolks with the granulated sugar until the mixture foams. Add the cream. Pour it into a large mold; it should be two fingers deep.

Preheat the oven to 375°. Set the mold in a pan half-filled with warm water and place it in the oven. Bake for 30 minutes or until set.

Leave the cream to cool in a cold place. Sprinkle it with the praline or brown sugar and place it under a preheated broiler for 2–3 minutes to melt and make a caramel topping. Leave in a cool place and serve cold.

Baked Bananas

Bananes au gratin

Serves 6

6 bananas
⅓ cup confectioner's sugar
2 tablespoons lemon juice
2 tablespoons melted unsalted butter

Preheat the oven to 400°. Slice the bananas in four lengthwise. Arrange them in a shallow greased ovenproof dish. Combine the confectioner's sugar, lemon juice and butter, and pour half of this sauce over the bananas. Bake for 20 minutes, basting with the rest of the sauce every 5 minutes. Serve hot or cold.

Cherry Bread

Pain de cerises

Serves 4

5 tablespoons flour
¼ teaspoon salt
5 cups (1 pound) cherries, pitted
½ cup unsalted butter, diced

Preheat the oven to 375°. Combine the flour, 2 cups water, and the salt, and mix this with the cherries. Grease a shallow ovenproof dish and pour the mixture into it. Sprinkle with the little cubes of butter. Bake for just under 1 hour or until browned.

Apples with Pistachios

Pommes aux pistaches

Serves 6

1 cup sugar
1 vanilla bean
6 apples, peeled and cored
1 cup pistachio nuts, shelled and peeled

Heat the sugar and 1 cup water in a heavy pan. Add the vanilla bean. When the syrup boils, add the apples. Cook, basting with the syrup, for 10 minutes.

Remove the apples and let them cool before putting them on a serving platter. Stick the pistachio nuts into the apples. Continue cooking the syrup until it thickens but do not let it color. Pour it over the apples. Let the apples cool and serve cold.

Apple Meringue

Pommes meringuées

This recipe is also very good when prunes are added to the stewed apple.

Serves 6

10 tart apples, peeled, cored and sliced
1 cup sugar
2 egg whites
2 tablespoons sugar
1 tablespoon grated lemon rind

Stew the apples in 1 cup sugar and water to cover. Preheat the oven to 300°. Pour the stewed apples into an ovenproof dish, mounding them into a pyramid. Beat the egg whites, and when they are beginning to stiffen, beat in the sugar and lemon rind. Pile on top of the apples. Bake for 15 minutes or until the meringue is firm and just beginning to color. Serve hot.

Chocolate Creams

Crème au chocolat

Serves 6

4 ½ cups milk
2½ cups (8 ounces) grated semisweet chocolate
⅔ cup sugar
5 egg yolks
1 egg

Pour ½ cup of the milk into a saucepan and heat it over low heat. Add the grated chocolate and stir to melt. Gradually add the rest of the milk, and the sugar, stirring constantly with a wooden spoon. Remove the mixture from the heat and let it cool. Beat the yolks with

the whole egg and beat this into the mixture. Strain it through cheesecloth or a fine sieve.

Preheat the oven to 350°. Pour the cream into 6 little molds. Set these in a pan half-filled with warm water and bake for 30 minutes or until set.

Flamed Apples

Pommes flambées

Serves 4

1 cup sugar
4 apples, peeled and cored
4 tablespoons raspberry or blackcurrant preserves
4 tablespoons cognac, warmed

Put the sugar and 1 cup water into a heavy pan and bring to a boil without stirring. Boil for 5 minutes, then add the apples. Cook for 10 minutes.

Remove the apples, continuing to cook the syrup, and place them on the serving dish. Fill the holes in the center with the preserves. Reduce the syrup for another 10 minutes until it has thickened but not colored and pour it over the apples. Pour the warmed cognac over them and flame.

Bananas in Red Wine

Daube de bananes

Serves 6

4 tablespoons unsalted butter
6 bananas, split lengthwise
3 cups dry red wine
3 tablespoons confectioner's sugar
¼ teaspoon ground cinnamon

Melt the butter in a skillet and add the bananas. Sauté them until they are golden, turning to cook on both sides. Remove and reserve them. Pour the wine into a large saucepan with the confectioner's sugar and cinnamon. Boil it over medium to low heat for 10 minutes, then add the bananas and simmer for 10 minutes. Serve hot.

Banana Ice Cream

La glace à la banane

Serves 6

2 cups milk
¼ teaspoon salt
5 egg yolks
2 cups confectioner's sugar
1 teaspoon cornstarch
4 bananas
⅔ cup heavy cream or crème fraîche

At least 15 minutes before it is to be used, prepare a hand-cranked ice cream maker by filling it with layers of crushed ice and sea salt with salt-peter.

To make the basic mixture, scald the milk with a pinch of salt. Meanwhile, put the egg yolks, sugar and cornstarch in a bowl. Beat well with a wooden spoon until the mixture is white and foaming. Incorporate a little of the hot milk, while stirring. Pour the mixture into a copper pan and add the rest of the milk. Cook over low heat, stirring constantly, until the mixture thickens but does not boil. As soon as the mixture coats the back of a spoon, remove it from the heat. Let it cool.

Peel the bananas and mash them with a fork to make a purée. Pass them through a fine sieve and incorporate this purée into the cooled mixture. Gradually add the cream, beating gently with a wire whip.

Pour the mixture into the ice cream maker. Cover it with a circle of waxed paper than add the lid. Crank the handle of the ice cream maker for 30 minutes until the ice cream begins to freeze.

Open the ice cream maker and remove the frozen mixture. Press it into the mold you have chosen to use, preferably a sugarloaf-shaped (conical) mold. Pack the ice cream into the mold, using a wooden spoon to remove any air cavities. Cover the open end of the mold with a circle of waxed paper. Place it in a narrow bucket partly filled with ice and salt. Leave for 1 hour to set. Just before serving, remove the mold from the bucket, and hold it under cold water, then dip it into hot water. Turn it out onto a napkin placed on the serving platter.

To Preserve Whole Bunches of Grapes

Pour conserver les grappes de raisins

Hang each bunch from a string, outdoors if it is sunny, and, if not, in the storeroom. They need heat and no humidity. If they are preserved indoors, they need to be in an airy spot. Remove any grapes which are damaged.

To Make Raisins from Grapes

Pour sêcher les raisins

Boil a handful of wood ash in water to cover for 2 hours. Filter the water through cheesecloth. Return it to the heat and boil it until it is reduced. Dip undamaged grapes in it. Begin with just one bunch, and if the grapes do not wrinkle up immediately, boil the water longer. Rinse the grapes in cold water, then hang them up in a dry, airy place. When the raisins are to be used, wash them in fresh water several times, then leave them to swell in warm water.

Opposite: Banana
ice cream was served
after the huge
Christmas lunch
(recipe on this page).

Teas

Chestnut Cookies

Galettes aux marrons

Makes 20

½ cup unsalted butter
1 cup unsweetened chestnut purée
¾ cup sugar
3 eggs, separated

Grease 20 cupcake molds. Preheat the oven to 350°. Melt the butter over low heat and stir in the chestnut purée, sugar and egg yolks. Remove the pan from the heat. Beat the egg whites into stiff peaks and fold them into the mixture. Divide the mixture among the molds and bake for 20 minutes, or until firm.

Genoa Cake

Pain de Gênes

Serves 12

½ cup unsalted butter, softened
1½ cups confectioner's sugar
5 eggs
2¼ cups ground almonds
2 tablespoons kirsch
⅔ cup flour
½ cup sifted confectioner's sugar (optional)
1 cup slivered almonds (optional)

Grease a shallow 8-inch cake pan. Preheat the oven to 350°. Cream the butter in a bowl and beat in the sugar, beating until the mixture is creamy. Continue beating while incorporating the eggs, one at a time, beating well after each addition. Beat in the ground almonds with the kirsch. Finally, add the flour and beat well. Pour into the prepared pan and bake for 40 minutes or until golden. If desired, sprinkle with sifted confectioner's sugar and top with slivered almonds.

Rich Fruit Cake

Cake

Serves 8

3 tablespoons unsalted butter
3 tablespoons sugar
2 eggs
2 tablespoons rum
1 cup mixed dried fruit, chopped
1¼ cups flour

Grease an 8-inch cake pan. Preheat the oven to 325°. Soften the butter in a bain-marie or double boiler. Remove the bowl from the heat and beat in the sugar. Add the eggs one after the other, beating well after each addition. Add the rum and the dried fruit. Gradually beat in the flour. Pour the mixture into the cake pan and bake for at least 20 minutes, or until a knife inserted into the center comes out clean.

Scones

Scones

Makes about 20

2 cups flour
1 teaspoon baking powder
¼ teaspoon salt
About 5 ounces milk
4 tablespoons butter

Sift the flour with the baking powder and salt. Rub in the butter. Add enough milk to make a rather soft dough. Roll out the dough until it is about ½ inch thick.

Preheat the oven to 400°. Cut out circles with a thin glass and place them on a greased baking sheet. Bake for 15 minutes or until well-risen and lightly browned. Serve hot, slicing them in half crosswise and buttering them.

Opposite: Monet's favorites for tea were scones, chestnut cookies, Genoa cake, and rich fruit cake (recipes on this page).

Honey Cookies

Palets au miel

Makes 15

2 eggs
1 cup confectioner's sugar
¼ cup honey
1 ¼ cups flour

Combine the eggs and sugar, beating hard for at least 5 minutes. Add the honey and mix well, and beat in the flour gradually. Let the mixture rest for 30 minutes.

Grease a baking sheet. Preheat the oven to 300°. Use a teaspoon to place small mounds of the mixture on the baking sheet. Bake for 15 minutes, or until the cookies are golden-brown.

Millet's Bread Rolls

Petits pains (Millet)

Makes 29

1 cup milk
5 teaspoons sugar
1 teaspoon salt
2 ½ tablespoons butter
1 scant tablespoon fresh yeast or 1 envelope dried yeast
4 cups flour
2 eggs, beaten
1 egg yolk, mixed with 3 tablespoons milk

Heat the milk with the sugar to just below a boil. Leave it to cool to lukewarm. Add the salt and butter. Meanwhile, in a bowl sprinkle the yeast over 1 cup warm water. Stir in 4 tablespoons flour. Leave in a warm place for 20 minutes, by which time the mixture should be spongy. Add the rest of the flour.

Mix the lukewarm milk mixture with the eggs. Beat the mixture into the flour mixture with a wooden spoon, then knead by hand, until the dough is smooth and elastic, and no longer sticks to the sides of the bowl.

Sprinkle flour on a board and knead the dough on it

for another 5 minutes. Use a warmed knife to cut the dough into 29 pieces and roll each of these into the shape of a fat cigar, about 1 inch by 3 inches.

Place the pieces of dough in a warm place in the kitchen, cover with a damp cloth and leave for 3 hours.

Preheat the oven to 450°. Flour 2 baking sheets. Place the pieces of dough on the baking sheets and brush them with the egg yolk and milk mixture. Bake the bread rolls for 10 minutes.

Cinnamon Toast

Toasts à la canelle

Makes 12

¾ cup unsalted butter, softened
¾ cup sugar
5 teaspoons ground cinnamon
12 slices bread

Preheat the oven to 450°. Work the butter, sugar, and ground cinnamon into a smooth paste. Spread the mixture evenly over the slices of bread. Arrange the slices on a baking sheet and bake for 10 minutes, or until the butter bubbles. Serve hot.

Orange Cake

Gâteau à l'orange

Serves 6–8

½ cup sugar
2 eggs, separated
Juice of 1 orange, strained
¾ cup ground almonds
¾ cup flour

Grease an 8-inch cake pan. Preheat the oven to 325°. Beat the sugar and egg yolks together so that the mixture foams. Gradually beat in the strained orange juice, almonds and flour. Beat the egg whites into stiff peaks and fold them into the mixture. Pour the mixture into the cake pan and bake for 30 minutes.

Madeleines

Madeleines au citron

Makes 12

1 ¼ cups sugar
½ cup unsalted butter, softened
4 eggs, separated
1 cup flour
Grated rind of 1 lemon

Lightly grease and flour 12 madeleine molds. In a bowl, combine the sugar, butter and egg yolks, beating well until the mixture turns pale. Beat the egg whites into soft peaks. Gradually add the butter mixture to the whites, alternately with 1 tablespoon of the flour, until the mixture and the flour are used up.

Preheat the oven to 400°. Place a teaspoon of the mixture in each mold. Bake for 10 to 15 minutes, but no longer, or the madeleines will be too dry.

Caroline's Pancakes

Crêpes (Caroline)

The eggs can be separated and the whites beaten into peaks before incorporating in the batter.

Serves 10

2 cups flour
About 2 cups milk
About 3 eggs
1 tablespoon vegetable oil
½ cup unsalted butter

Make the batter 3 hours ahead of time, combining all the ingredients except the butter. If it seems too thin, add an egg; if it seems too thick, add more milk.

To cook the pancakes, heat an omelet or crêpe pan over high heat and melt 1 tablespoon butter in it, shaking the pan to coat it evenly. Drop enough batter into the pan to make 1 thin crêpe and cook quickly. Flip the pancake over with a metal spatula. Turn out onto a dish and reserve in a warm place. Continue making pancakes until all the butter and batter are used up.

Almond Cookies

Gâteaux nantais

Makes 40

4 cups flour
2 cups confectioner's sugar
½ cup unsalted butter, softened
1 cup ground almonds
Grated rind of 1 lemon
4 eggs
8 tablespoons chopped almonds
1 cup sugar

Grease two baking sheets. Preheat the oven to 325°. Pour the flour in a bowl and make a well in the center. Pour the confectioner's sugar into the center, and add the butter, ground almonds, lemon rind and eggs. Mix well. When the dough is smooth but firm, roll it out on a floured work surface into a rectangle about ½ inch thick. Cut into circles with a cookie cutter; transfer to the baking sheets. Sprinkle with the chopped almonds and sugar. Bake for 20 minutes or until golden.

French Toast

Pain perdu

Serves 4

2 eggs, beaten
½ cup milk
2 tablespoons confectioner's sugar
2 tablespoons rum
4 slices day-old brioche
4 tablespoons butter
½ cup granulated sugar

Pour the beaten eggs into a shallow bowl. Combine the milk with the confectioner's sugar and rum. Pour it into another shallow bowl. Soak the slices of brioche in the milk mixture. As soon as they are soaked, dip the slices on both sides in the beaten egg.

Melt the butter in a skillet. Sauté the slices in the butter, until browned on both sides. Serve hot, generously sprinkled with the granulated sugar.

Jams

Plum Jam

Confiture de prunes

Apricot jam can be made in the same way as plum jam.

Makes about 3 cups

3 cups granulated sugar
1 pound plums, halved and pitted

Pour the sugar and ½ cup water into a copper canning kettle. Bring to a boil, stirring only until the sugar has dissolved. Boil for 5 minutes, then add enough plums to cover the bottom of the kettle. They are cooked when they are transparent and when they will soften when pressed with the handle of a wooden spoon.

Remove the kettle from the heat, and use a fork to remove the plums from the kettle. Place them in canning jars. Return the kettle to the heat and bring the syrup to a rolling boil again. Place more plums in the kettle, and repeat the procedure, until all the plums are used up. Put the syrup back on the heat and pour any syrup remaining in the jars back into the kettle. Boil it again and pour it into the pots, making sure you dislodge the plums so that the syrup penetrates everywhere.

Uncooked Red Currant Jelly

Gelée de groseille à froid

Makes about 3 cups

5 cups (1 pound) red currants
About 2 cups sugar

Press the red currants through cheesecloth to extract the juice; the juice must be pure. Weigh the juice and weigh out the same amount of sugar.

Gradually pour the juice into the sugar, a few drops at a time, beating with a metal spoon, as for mayonnaise. When the sugar is well mixed with the juice, continue stirring for another 20 minutes.

Pour the mixture into prepared canning jars, still stirring. It is easier if there are two of you to do this. Put the jars, uncovered, in a cool, dry place. Leave them uncovered for 2 days, then cover and seal them.

Preserves

Cherry Preserves

Conserves de cerises

Fruits that yield a lot of juice such as red currants, gooseberries, cherries, and strawberries must be packed into the canning jars so that they completely fill them. These fruits need very little water. Fill the jars and close them with the hooked metal attachment. Place a cloth in the bottom of a deep canning kettle and half-fill the kettle with water. Place the jars upright in the kettle, so that the water comes up to the necks. Cover the kettle and put it over medium heat until it boils slowly; cherries will require 20 minutes' cooking time. This is an indispensable precaution to prevent the jars from breaking. After cooking, leave the jars to cool in the water. If they have been cooked enough, the covers will be sealed hermetically.

Brandied Cherries

Cerises à l'eau-de-vie

Makes 3 cups

5 cups (1 pound) cherries, stalks trimmed in half
½ cup granulated sugar
White brandy (marc)

Pack the cherries into canning jars, add the sugar and fill the jars with the alcohol. Seal the jars. It is not necessary to leave them in the sun, any more than it is with other fruits. They will take approximately two months to mature.

Left: Bottled summer fruits, including Marguerite's famous brandied cherries.

GENERAL INDEX

Page numbers in italics refer to photographic captions.

185

RECIPES INDEX

Page numbers in italics refer to photographic captions.

Claude Monet c.1920.